The Legacy
of
John Lennon

"What can parents expect during this decade as rock music advocates sadism, masochism, incest, necrophilia, homosexuality, bestiality, rape and violence in addition to the ever present rebellion, drug abuse and promiscuity? The obvious answer is stupifying."

Kingsbury Smith
National Editor
The Hearst Newspapers

The Legacy
of
John Lennon

Charming
or
Harming
a Generation?

by
David A. Noebel

Thomas Nelson Publishers
Nashville · Camden · New York

Published in Nashville, Tennessee, by Thomas Nelson, Inc. and distributed in Canada by Lawson Falle, Ltd., Cambridge, Ontario.

Printed in the United States of America.

ISBN 0-8407-4106-5 (cloth)
      0-8407-5786-7 (paperback)

Rock 'n' Roll Jet

Hello, my name is Rock 'n' Roll
And of people just like you
I always take a high toll
For I covet you see
Damnation, to your soul
So listen well
Since my time is closing
Enjoy my beat
And dips and swells
Yes, enjoy my melody
As I take you through
The gates of hell
I'll sift your minds
With vulgar rhymes
Cause my far-out beat
Carries brainwashing heat
Hot lust and bonding passion
Yearning burning aggravation
Yes by my words
I'll scorch your brain
And chuck your morals
Down the drain
Sure
I'm cutting you down
But I'm so good
You'll stick around
You dig my beat
So dance you clown
I'm going to laugh

When you're cast down
Dance, dance, dance
To my sweet romance
I'm bending your mind
Into a trance
Mmmm, I'm gonna make
A fag outa you
Or maybe
A crazy
Murderer will do
Or would you like
To be a rapist
Or how bout joining
The psycho cases
Either way
I don't care
So long as we have
Our affair
My groovy beat
My nerve jam tunes
Are for your soul
You dumb baboon
Get it, get it
Get down with me
Get way on down
And do your own thing
Mock those goofy
  churchy threats
And ride with me

Your Rock 'n' Roll jet
I'll swing your senses
To new releases
For I'm the pied piper
The teenage boogie
Ordered by Baal
To escort you
And give hell's path
A special appeal
So come along with me
And hurry please
Our time is short

And I so desire
To sing to you
By eternal fire
But when doomsday comes
I'll change my words
And turn up the beat
Cause then I'll have you
I'll have you
For eternal keeps.

Phil Barber

Contents

This book is dedicated to a fifteen-year-old boy named Randy who could not cope with rock music and drugs. May his tragic, senseless, early death be an example to others not to imitate his mistakes. May God rest his soul in peace. May God stir our souls to action to prevent further tragedies like Randy's.

"The human soul longs for things higher, warmer and purer than those offered by today's . . . intolerable music."

Alexander Solzhenitsyn
Harvard University
June 8, 1978

Introduction

On December 8, 1980, bullets ended the phenomenal life of former Beatle John Lennon. His violent death at age forty stunned millions of followers.

He left behind his wife, Yoko Ono, a son, and a staggering monetary legacy estimated at $275 million—not bad for one who referred to himself as an "instinctive socialist,"[1] for one who believed in the abolition of "all money, police, and government."[2]

Lennon's British holdings totaled $5.5 million, his American holdings, $30 million. In addition, his estate receives $12 million a year in royalties from his 25 percent ownership of Apple Records. His estate also receives $222,000 daily from a posthumous boom in record sales.

Newspaper columnist Patrick Buchanan added it up and said,

> At a simple 10 percent per year, his wealth would have earned him $27.5 million a year. The royalties from his records alone will pick up an additional $80 million in 1981—more money for Yoko Ono in one year, far more, than the top 80 oil executives of the Seven Sisters combined.[3]

Lennon owned dairy farms in upstate New York, Vermont, and Virginia. His 250 head of registered Holstein cattle were valued at $66 million. He owned five apartments in The Dakota, across from Manhattan's Central Park. He owned a $700,000 beachfront home in Palm Beach, Florida, which formerly belonged to the Vanderbilts. Lennon also owned a $450,000 gabled mansion in Cold Spring Harbor, Long Island, where the rock star moored his sixty-two foot yacht. And these were just his American holdings!

Not even Yoko Ono knew exactly what belonged to her. She felt it would take ten accountants "two years to find out what we have."[4]

Apart from leaving all his wealth behind, however, Lennon left something of far greater consequence—a cultural legacy institutionalized through rock 'n' roll. The crucial import of this legacy demands attention. Lennon's influence can be linked to our present atheistic, hedonistic culture, a culture that mimics his personal, social, religious, and ethical philosophy.

"Lennon's influence didn't stop with music," said Vern Stephanic. "He was more than a musician. He was a social activist. It was natural that as the Beatles rocketed to fame, Lennon would be the one most quoted and most listened to. He was the leader."[5]

Witnessing the eulogies to Lennon, however, it appeared that America had lost one of her finest sons. Hourly broadcasts of his hymn to humanism "Imagine" became an overnight ritual. The airwaves were monopolized by his drug, sex, and social protest music. It was impressive and incessant. "The deification of John Lennon by the mass media," said Dr. Max Rafferty, "only proves the complete desperation of Western culture."[6]

Rafferty, former Secretary of Public Education in the

state of California, described the whole rock 'n' roll culture thusly:

> It stands to reason that a system of entertainment which blasted eardrums into a state of permanent disrepair, which featured performers who looked like fugitives from a horror movie and who brayed like Balaam's original ass, and which staged 'festivals' at which killings were common and mass orgies part of the ritual just had to be as corrupt and depraved as, in fact, it looked and sounded.[7]

Meanwhile, on the other side of the globe, Big Brother was also eulogizing Lennon. The Soviet press, according to *New York Times* writer Anthony Austin, was heaping lavish praise on him. They had not forgotten his odes to atheism, socialism, and Angela Davis. They remembered his role in neutralizing America's involvement in the Vietnam War and his support of the Students for a Democratic Society (SDS) and the Irish Republican Army (IRA). The Soviet press referred to Lennon as "a fighter for peace."[8] Some years earlier *Pravda*, the official voice of the Kremlin, praised Lennon because "he likes the Soviet Union very much."[9] *Pravda* knew that such statements by popular teenage idols had a significant impact on youth.

The purpose of this book is to reveal the ideology propounded by John Lennon and the Beatles. It is imperative that we realize what our youth are following and why.

Interestingly, the truth about Lennon *has* been published. Lennon himself acknowledged that Michael Brown's book *Love Me Do* was a true book because it portrayed the Beatles "as [expletive deleted]. [Expletive deleted] big [expletive deleted]"[10] which, according to

Lennon, was exactly what they were. Such honesty did not make the evening news!

American media, however, always had a difficult time telling the truth about Lennon and the Beatles. When Yoko Ono once asked John how the Beatles were able to keep such a clean image in spite of all the evidence to the contrary, he casually replied, "Everybody wants the image to carry on. You want to carry on. The press is around too, because they want the free drinks, and the free whores, and the fun."[11]

Recently *US* magazine published a ninety-eight page special edition on the life and times of John Lennon. Portions of the preceding material never made it into the magazine. Instead, we are informed "the Lennons championed many social causes and were happy together."[12] The way *US* magazine and the press in general handled John Lennon is comparable to describing Judas as a disciple of Jesus, but failing to mention the crucial fact that he betrayed the Lord.

America's youth are bombarded with bizarre themes rhythmically hidden within the rock 'n' roll cultural matrix. Lennon and the Beatles supplied this receptive pop culture with lyric approval for dirt, drugs, and social rebellion. Formerly taboo perversions and the occult spice up their songs or the songs of their followers.

The assault on Western values has been absolutely fierce. It is moral war! The undeclared battle to subvert the values of our youth is without parallel, so far as I know, in the history of the world.

Yet the media continue to idolize rock stars who sing about sexual anarchy, drugged oblivion, and emotional destruction. It would appear that the media have pledged support to hasten the crumbling of the moral order.

Neither John Lennon nor his legacy is ethically attractive. John Lennon was a purveyor of moral trash, a drug connoisseur, a driving force of the revolution. His first wife, Cynthia, avows that their marriage deteriorated when Lennon laced their relationship with LSD and marijuana.[13] And one must question why *Rolling Stone* magazine commemorated Lennon seven weeks after his death with a nude cover photo (January 22, 1981).

The present rock 'n' roll scene, Lennon's legacy, is one giant, multi-media portrait of degradation—a sleezy world of immorality, venereal disease, anarchy, nihilism, cocaine, heroin, marijuana, death, Satanism, perversion, and orgies.

Although Lennon is dead, his legacy continues to seduce yet another generation of immature, impressionable youth into the evil vortex of rock 'n' roll and its subculture.

One

The Issue

The message is drugs. The message is sex. The message is drugs and sex.

Sound familiar?

It should! The drug and sexual revolutions, spawned as social protest on our college campuses little more than a decade or so ago, filtered down to our high schools, our junior high schools, even our grade schools. The implications are staggering.

Teenage pregnancies are epidemic.[1] One million unwed teenage girls—one out of ten—are made pregnant every year. A 1977 study shows that approximately 600,000 unwed teenagers were giving birth each year. Thirty-eight percent abort![2] Venereal disease is out of control, with one million reported cases of gonorrhea and one-half million cases of herpes every year. Fifty percent of the nation's 10 million young women aged fifteen through nineteen have experienced premarital sex. "I'd say half the girls in my graduating class are virgins," says eighteen-year-old Sharon Bernard, a high school senior. "But you wouldn't believe those freshmen and sophomores. By the time they graduate there aren't going to be any virgins left."[3]

Although teenage sex is a major problem, it dwarfs in

comparison to the teenage drug problem. Millions of children, many aged ten years and under, are habitual users of marijuana, barbituates, and hallucinogens. Thousands die every year from drug overdoses or drug-related accidents or incidents.[4]

Many high schools and junior high schools are becoming drug centers. Students are getting "stoned" on the way to school, during school, after school, and at home (where they often use incense to cover the smell).

A 1978 high school senior survey disclosed that one out of nine seniors smoked pot (marijuana) daily. Of that group, forty percent used additional illegal drugs. Another study revealed that the use of marijuana is twice as high for youngsters as for adults. And one in ten pot-smoking youngsters used stronger drugs.

Drugs are so prevalent among teens today that high schools are often rated by the number of students taking dope. If a high school is a fifty percenter, it means that about half the students are on drugs. Some high schools are ninety percenters!

Congressman Lester Wolff (D-N.Y.), chairman of the House Select Committee on Narcotics Abuse and Control, insists that our nation is the most pervasive drug abusing nation in history:

> Drug abuse among our children has risen, in the past two years, from epidemic to pandemic proportions. It has grown so large that neither the nation—nor any nation in history—has ever before faced a problem that is so insidious and so dangerous. And if we don't recognize the importance of this problem, it will have disastrous effects upon our society.[5]

Another expert on the drug problem, Lee Dogoloff, former White House drug policy adviser, warns what might happen if the present adolescent drug-abuse trends continue:

> We could soon acquire an unmanageable number of emotionally, intellectually and socially handicapped young people. We could have a 'diminished generation' unable to function effectively, if at all, in an increasingly complex and demanding world. In the area of adolescent drug abuse, therefore, we have neither the luxury of time nor the opportunity for esoteric debate.[6]

How did we ever get ourselves into such a predicament? We accepted and embraced rock 'n' roll music as a plus, a positive, a good, an innocent form of musical entertainment.

The truth is that rock 'n' roll is a moral hemlock. It is by nature a music of demonic rebellion and protest. Drugs and sex are its arsenal. Altamont, the rock festival in California, where rock 'n' roll ruled supreme (where, by association, drugs and sex reigned), proved that rock is not a harbinger of love, joy, and peace. Rather, it is the accompaniment of evil and violence.

Newsweek, in a review of the motion picture "The Rose" starring Bette Midler, summarized the film in its very first line—"Drugs, sex, *and rock 'n' roll*" [italics added].[7]

The twenty-five-year history of rock music is the history of drugs and sex. Early rock star Little Richard said, "I was using dope, marijuana, angel dust, cocaine and heroin with pills and drinking. All I wanted to do was have orgies, get high and sing all my old hits."[8]

Our young people are high on drugs and sex because their music is high on drugs and sex. Could it be any different? "For the reality of what's happening today in America," says Ralph J. Gleason, "we must go to rock 'n' roll."[9]

Kingsbury Smith, national editor of the Hearst newspapers, said:

> What can parents expect during this decade as rock music advocates sadism, masochism, incest, necrophilia, homosexuality, bestiality, rape and violence in addition to the ever present rebellion, drug abuse and promiscuity? The obvious answer is stupifying.[10]

Former *New York Times* writer McCandlish Phillips acknowledges that our youth culture is "shot through with the philosophy of Satan." There is, he says,

> ceaseless, incessant, pounding progaganda in the ears and eyes of the young, promoting fornication, mysticism (the occult), marijuana, and violent revolution, and we are at the point where young women seek roles as "urban guerrillas" and others feel "pregnant with murder."[11]

Phillips says such behavior is "earthly, sensual, devilish" and the purpose behind it is destructive—individually and nationally! "Satan and the demons have created a quagmire for the young"—easy sex, drugs, the occult, and participation in revolution. "Now they are urging them to march into it by the masses, and they are supplying the lyrics, the drumbeat, and the tune."[12]

The masses are marching into the drug culture, the sex scene, the cultural revolution; the rock stars are supplying the drumbeat, the tune, and the words. "Van Halen Lives, Pushes Sex, Drugs, and Rock 'n' Roll" proclaimed a headline in the *Tampa Tribune*.[13] The article said that although Ian Dury wrote the words, "Sex and drugs and rock 'n' rock is all my brain and body needs," the group Van Halen seems to live them. Ten thousand screaming fans bought every ticket to the concert and were carefully fed a diet of moral arsenic. Says the *Tribune*, "by playing to the lowest common denominator—partying—singer David Lee Roth allied the audience with the band against authority by constantly saying how great it was that everybody was 'messed up' from drug and alcohol abuse."[14]

In a recent NBC News special entitled "Reading, Writing, and Reefer," Edwin Newman interviewed young teenagers who admitted their lives revolved around smoking dope and listening to rock music.

Suggestive rock music, such as "Take Your Time (Do It Right)" and "Do That to Me One More Time," climbs high on the charts.

Dr. Bryon Hawkes' assessment is that the apparent sexual anarchy among American youth is "Partly the outcome of living in a society in which kids are continually bombarded with sexually suggestive messages . . . They can't listen to a rock 'n' roll band and not hear suggestive passages."[15] The relationship between drugs, sex, and rock 'n' roll is becoming clearer. In an article headlined "Teens Cheer Rights Leader,"

> The Rev. Jesse Jackson ripped into the drug culture, easy sex and 'pornographic music' during a speech to 14,000 high school students who gave him a frenzied, gospel-like standing ovation. Today's music aimed at the teenage audience is "nothing but pornography." You cannot be somebody and blow your minds on this type of music. This stuff is short-term pleasure and long-term payments.[16]

It is now payment time. We are reaping what has been sown for more than two decades. There is a law of sowing and reaping. Each year thousands of young people die from drug overdoses, drug-related accidents, and drug-induced suicide. Twenty million already have the incurable venereal disease herpes.

Yet the musicians and promoters who create the environment for this human destruction continue to sell millions of records.

We cannot continue to ignore the powerful influence of music for good or for evil. We need to heed Plato's observation that "musical training is a more potent instrument than any other, because rhythm and harmony find their way into the inward places of the soul, on which they mightily fasten."[17]

Music is the most effective mood influence in existence. Few men and women are neutral toward the excitement of the "Washington Post March," "Stars and Stripes Forever," "The Marine Hymn," or "Anchors Aweigh" as they observe a Fourth of July parade.

Few churchgoers can resist the soul-stirring inspiration of "Blest Be the Tie That Binds," "He Lives," "Just As I Am," "Amazing Grace," or "Holy, Holy, Holy" as they join a congregation in worship.

Babies find peace, confidence, and solace in the soft lullaby. People of all ages, races, and social backgrounds thrill to the music of Beethoven, Mozart, Bach—and the same people enjoy the rollicking refrains of musical comedies and the catchy rhythms of spirituals and camp meeting songs.

Music is a rich part of the American tradition, and its role is portrayed vividly by Dr. Samuel Eliot Morrison in his *Oxford History of the American People*. Ending each chapter of American history with a fitting song from that period, Dr. Morrison includes such timeless favorites as "Am I a Soldier of the Cross," "Hail Columbia," "Dixie Land," "Battle Hymn of the Republic," "Tenting Tonight," "Oh, How I Hate to Get Up in the Morning," "Of Thee I Sing," and "Camelot."

"Music," said William Congreve, "has charms to

soothe the savage breast." It also can stir up the savage breast! "Music," said Dr. Howard Hanson, "has powers for evil as well as for good."

Jacques Barzun's work *Darwin, Marx, Wagner* dispels any slight to the importance of music as a cultural preparation for certain ideas.

Richard Wagner, at one time a socialist, boasted, "My task is this: to bring revolution wherever I go."[18] Barzun's thesis is that it was no accident that during the "Wagner era" the ideas of Darwin and Marx swept Europe and England. Wagner, a poet and composer, set the cultural stage for acceptance of such ideas.

Similarly, rock 'n' roll is setting today's stage for the acceptance of drugs, promiscuity, V.D., and revolution. This is doubtless what Martin Perlich meant when he said, "Wagner was happy to describe his music as tribal and revolutionary, and this is exactly what current rock music is."[19]

This book will examine the cultural phenomenon plaguing our youth and offer suggestions for rescuing our children from rock 'n' roll's dead end. Make no mistake—drugs, permissiveness, the occult, and suicide are emotional, mental, spiritual, and physical dead ends.

The rock phenomenon spells tragedy, violence, foolishness, darkness, and despair.

When we are informed that rock music is "the music of rebellion against parents and against moral restraints,"[20] it is time to sit up and take notice.

And when we are told that if we really knew what rock music is saying, "not what the words are saying, but the music itself is saying, we'd ban it, smash it and arrest anyone who tried to play it."[21] It is past time to come to grips with the subject.

This book describes a malady that makes the bubonic plague (which wiped out one-third of fourteenth century Europe) look like a health spa. It also describes the absurdity, meaninglessness, incredulity, darkness, and despair facing us if we retreat or surrender.

C.S. Lewis warned:

> As Christians we are tempted to make unnecessary concessions to those outside the Faith. We give in too much. . . . We must show our Christian colours if we are to be true to Jesus Christ. We cannot remain silent and concede everything away.[22]

Hopefully, this work will feed the spirit with truth wrapped in love.

Two

The Image

Observing the evolution of rock 'n' roll from its beginning through the present, we can understand why rock star Little Richard said, "Rock 'n' roll is devastating to the mind."[1]

But he further admits, "Rock 'n' roll doesn't glorify God. You can't drink out of God's cup and the devil's cup at the same time. I was one of the pioneers of that music, one of the builders. I know what the blocks are made of because I built them."[2]

Little Richard helped write an early chapter in the Beatles saga. In 1962 Brian Epstein,[3] manager of the Beatles, convinced Little Richard to let his new unknown group share the bill at a Liverpool, England, club with Little Richard and his rock musicians, Jimi Hendrix and Billy Preston. Said Little Richard, "They [the Beatles] were little, strange-looking fellows. They all had their little bangs."[4]

Strange-looking or not, within a few years the influence of the Beatles was felt throughout the world. Why? Youth were fascinated by their unconventional manner and music, "I am he as you are he as you are me and we are all together."[5]

But the influence of Lennon and the Beatles is proving to be a negative influence on our youth! Lennon criticized Christianity, drug laws, America, Britain—anything he perceived as hostile to his world view.

When ministers counsel parents who have lost children to the rock-drug culture, it is difficult for them to maintain a neutral view toward rock music. But when ministers are called upon to bury fifteen- or sixteen-year-olds who committed suicide because they could not cope with the rock-drug culture, neutrality is no longer an option. Yet, it is nearly impossible to locate a rock group not living on drugs. "Working in the rock world and refusing to use cocaine are rather like joining a rugby club and preaching abstinence,"[6] said author Tony Sanchez.

Are those of us opposed to rock 'n' roll unduly negative? Bob Larson observed in his work *Rock:*

> Others may feel the analyses are slanted toward bringing out the negative aspects of rock artists without fairly drawing attention to more positive elements in their character and music. It should be obvious that what's good isn't a problem and doesn't need accentuation . . . It is the objectionable moral impact of these people with which we're concerned, and that is why this aspect is emphasized.[7]

It is heartening to know that some pro-rock critics acknowledge a grudging truth to the detractors. Robert W. Butler of the *Kansas City Times* wrote:

> The preachers and moral guardians who in rock's infancy warned us of the evils of the music weren't that far off base. Rock—at least as practiced by The Who and a few others—is defiant, it is antisocial, it is revolutionary . . . Anarchy, that's what The Who is all about.[8]

Former *New York Times* writer McCandlish Phillips analyzed characteristics of the new youth subculture—

minimum standard of dress, low standard of cleanliness, passivity toward productive work, repudiation of authority, lax sexual mores, acceptance of revolution, acceptance and dependence upon drugs, interest in the occult—and concluded:

> The Beatles were not responsible for it all by any means, but they began it, set some of its most obtrusive styles, rode it like a wild steed; and the Beatles made the big breakthrough into the West for yogism and Eastern mysticism. Altogether, trend-setting of potent impact on the young.[9]

Phillips also noted that the composite lyrics screamed, crooned, and moaned by the Beatles yield a philosophy devoid of character. The philosophy? The counsel of nihilism, instant gratification, rebellion, mystical dreamscapes, picturesque unreality, psychedelia, sex upbeat, narcotic upbeat, listlessness, hopelessness, stagnacy, apathy, lethargy, alternating cycles of stimulation and depression, "neither [sic] productive of any good."[10]

Our society will not be healed nor lives reclaimed by continuing to ignore rock's negative impact on our values. When Butler mentioned "rock's infancy," he could easily have included rock's present state, too! The history of rock over the past two decades reveals its debilitative nature. Or, as rock star David Bowie put it, "Rock and roll has always been the devil's music. It could well bring about a very evil feeling in the West."[11]

As Bowie was candid, so was Lennon. Lennon was far more truthful about himself, the Beatles, and rock music than most of the Western media. Lennon spoke the brutal truth—with media amnesty—on many, many subjects, and for that we must give credit where credit is due. "Who was going to knock us when there's a million pounds to be made?"[12] he asked.

Or again:

Everybody wanted in . . . Don't take it away from us, you know, don't take Rome from us, not a portable Rome where we can all have our houses and our cars and our lovers and our wives and office girls and parties and drinks and drugs.[13]

"We know what we are because we know what we're doing,"[14] said Lennon. *Lennon personally refuted those critics who believed the Beatles just innocently stumbled into certain situations.* "There were very few things that happened to the Beatles that weren't really well thought out by us whether to do it or not,"[15] continued Lennon.

When asked why rock 'n' roll meant so much to people, Lennon shot straight:

Because it is primitive enough and has no bull, really, the best stuff, and it gets through to you its beat. Go to the jungle and they have the rhythm and it goes throughout the world and it's as simple as that.[16]

Lennon did speak truth about love and sex—at least once! "I'm not going to sacrifice love, real love, for any whore," he said, "because in the end you're alone at night. You can't fill the bed with groupies, that doesn't work. I don't want to be a swinger. I've been through it all and nothing works better than to have somebody you love hold you."[17]

John Lennon also must be commended for fathering and loving Sean. In fact, after five years of parenting, Lennon again hit home.

The reason why kids are crazy is because nobody can face the responsibility of bringing them up. Everybody's too scared to deal with children all the time, so we reject them and send them away [to school] and torture them.[18]

Having said this about Lennon, however, we still must reckon with our present problems generated by the music unleashed by countless rock groups. Our youth are suffering. Lennon's legacy is powerful, and his legacy is evil.

Dr. Howard Hanson, formerly with the Eastman School of Music, University of Rochester, said:

Music is a curiously subtle art with innumerable, varying emotional connotations. It is made up of many ingredients and, according to the proportions of those components, it can be soothing or invigorating, ennobling or vulgarizing, philosophical or orgiastic. It has powers for evil as well as for good.[19]

Lennon, the Beatles, and rock 'n' roll all fall into the secondary categories of "invigorating," "vulgarizing," and "orgiastic"—and Hanson was writing in 1942, long before the age of rock!

Dr. Bernard Saibel, child guidance expert for the State of Washington's Division of Community Services described a 1964 Beatles concert attended by 14,000 teenagers. He called the experience "unbelievable and frightening." According to Saibel, "the hysteria and loss of control go far beyond the impact of the music." Many of those present became "frantic, hostile, uncontrolled, screaming, unrecognizable beings."

Saibel said the type of behavior was not simply a release, "but a very destructive process." It was a process of allowing the child to be involved in a mad, erotic world without reassuring safeguards and protection. Girls behaved as "if possessed by some demonic urge."

The music, said Saibel, was loud, primitive, insistent, and strongly rhythmic. It released in a "disguised way" the all too tenuously controlled, newly acquired physical impulses of the teenager.

He concluded by saying that regardless of the causes or reasons for the behavior of these youngsters, it had the impact of an unholy bedlam. "It was an orgy for teenagers."[20]

"The big beat is deliberately aimed at exciting the listener," said Dimitri Tiomkin, famous composer and conductor.

> There is actually very little melody, little sense in the lyrics, only rhythm. The fact that music can both excite and incite has been known from time immemorial. That was perhaps its chief function in prehistory and it remains so in the primitive societies which still exist in the far reaches of the world. In civilized countries, music became more and more a means of communicating pleasurable emotions, not creating havoc. Now in our popular music, at least, we seem to be reverting to savagery . . . and youngsters who listen constantly to this sort of sound are thrust into turmoil. They are no longer relaxed, normal kids.[21]

Compare Saibel's and Tiomkin's words with the following from Dr. Howard Hanson and Dr. William Sargant.

Said Hanson:

> The mass hysteria present in recordings of the rhythmic chants of primitive peoples and the similar mass hysteria of the modern 'jam session' indicates—at times, all too clearly—the emotional tension producible by subjecting groups of people to concentrated doses of rhythm.[22]

Dr. Sargant, head of the Psychological Medicine Department at St. Thomas Hospital in London, said in an address to the Royal Society of Medicine:

Adolf Hitler, ancient Greek orators, the Beatles and African witch doctors all practiced a similar type of brainwashing. I believe the human brain has not altered since the Stone Age. People can be brainwashed to believe sense or nonsense. You should be warned when young, of the way people get at you when you are older. Rhythmic music and dancing are ways of getting at the nervous system. (I will show some) movies demonstrating how the primitive rhythms of a Stone Age tribe in Kenya and a band at a London ball produce the same trancelike emotions . . . Hitler got people into a tremendous state of excitement and then talked to them. This method can be used for either good or evil. Hitler used it and killed twenty million people.[23]

Sid Bernstein agreed with the comparison, "Only Hitler ever duplicated their [the Beatles'] power over crowds."[24]

And *Time* magazine commented, "The fact remains that when the Beatles talk—about drugs, the war in Vietnam, religion—millions listen, and this is the new situation in the pop music world."[25]

"The battle lines involved much more than music," said rock critic Vern Stefanic. "It involved a drug culture, an anti-God theme, and anti-America, pro-revolution stance. It involved recognizing that Lennon was more than a musician."[26]

Millions of families suffer as their children become victims of the drug counterculture. Countless other families suffer from the consequences of the "new morality." And still more families fight to protect their children from rock's implicit permission to practice homosexuality and occultism.

For these families, the issue is clear. For millions of others, however, the relationship of rock music to illegal drugs and illicit sex is yet to be realized.

Three

The Culture

John Lennon's brief college career began at Liverpool Art College. It was here that he studied Vincent van Gogh, but not his hero Marcel Duchamp. "Duchamp was spot [sic] on," insisted Lennon, "He would just put a bike wheel on display and he would say this is art!"[1]

Duchamp is one of the greats in a group of artists who believe this world and this life to be absurd. Duchamp held that "all values, norms, forms, traditions, all that belonged to Western culture including its art, had lost their meaning."[2] He further looked for "a great upheaval, the breakdown of our culture, and the acceptance of nihilism and anarchism."[3]

Western culture with its attendant Christian values has been under attack for some time, however. "Our culture is breaking down," said H. R. Rookmaaker, "and if any confirmation is needed, go to the films, read the books of today, walk round a modern art gallery, listen to the music of our times."[4]

Dr. Max Rafferty believes that the arts tend to reflect the state of mind of the centuries. During the Middle Ages, for example, painting, sculpture, music and poetry mirrored the chief concern of the people—religion.

In answer to the question, what do the twentieth century arts reflect? he said:

> Painting depicts chaos—blobs of color apparently thrown at random upon the canvas. Sculpture is twisted junk from the nearest trash yard. Poetry is unintelligible. And music is punk rock. The arts say we're insane. Maybe the arts are right.[5]

It doesn't take much investigation or imagination to conclude that the current offerings of films, literature, art and music are anemic.

If a film isn't marked "X", "XXX", "R", or labeled "girlie," it stands little chance of survival. Homosexuality is being glorified in one way or another in some of the leading films being shown right now including "Making Love," "Partners," "Victor/Victoria," and "Personal Best." Patrick Buchanan attended Robert Altman's 1979 film, *A Wedding*. The two-hour plus movie depicts a single day in the lives of two American families. It opens with a shot of a cross, the symbol of Christianity, high inside a Catholic church where a marriage ceremony is being performed by a semi-senile bishop.

Buchanan summarized the motion picture in fourteen points, five of which are salient to this discussion: (1) the groom is a youthful lecher who impregnated his sister-in-law, the maid of honor, (2) the best man is a homosexual who tries to seduce the groom, (3) the mother of the bride spends most of the movie plotting adultery with an uncle, (4) the mother of the groom is a heroin addict, and (5) the maid of honor is a retarded nymphomaniac.

"Reflecting," said Buchanan, "it is difficult to recall a

single character who is not idiotic, sordid, or absurd. Nor can one locate a single value or character trait or institution that is defended or affirmed."[6]

And Buchanan questioned where we are headed "when this sort of solid waste is being poured by Hollywood directly into the mainstream of American culture without first being filtered through a sewage treatment facility."[7]

But if our films are cultural voids, consider briefly modern literature. "The literature of today lacks certain essential qualities," said Prof. Duncan Williams.

> It no longer satisfies man's need for beauty, order, and elevation. . . . It contains, as Trilling has observed, an anti-civilizing trend, and to this is closely linked a cult of ugliness, a morbid concentration on the baser elements of life, a clinical obsession with the bizarre, with the grossly sensual and degrading aspects of human culture.[8]

Williams described the total rejection of tradition, morality, and religion as the death throes of a culture. Specifically he charged that "For the vast majority of modern writers, artists, critics and other molders of public taste and beliefs, God in the old sense of the word, is not dead, but never existed."[9]

According to Williams, those who profess faith in God are either moral cowards or lack the intellectual apparatus to give their opinions weight.

To understand what is happening on the literary front, one must understand the secularization of Western culture. According to Williams, Sartre's existentialism and the Theatre of the Absurd "are all in differing ways manifestations of a failure to believe in a Supreme Being and, therefore, in a regulated, ordered universe."[10]

Literary giant Malcolm Muggeridge said of William's book:

> *Trousered Apes* is a cogently argued, highly intelligent and devastatingly effective anatomization of what passes for culture today, showing that it is nihilistic in purpose, ethically and spiritually vacuous and Gadarene in destination.[11]

The bitter 1974 textbook controversy in West Virginia reinforced Williams' and Muggeridge's observations. Although the media reported the struggle as ignorance versus intelligence, columnist Jeffrey St. John interpreted the essential issue as secularism versus religion, collectivism versus individualism—in reality a clash between two value systems. Said St. John, "The parents believe strongly in the fundamental teachings of the Bible and love of country, and closeness of family."[12]

A school board member remarked that the textbooks "were full of negative references to Christianity and God . . . lots of profanity and anti-American stories . . . literature encouraging stealing, disobedience of authority and sexual immorality."[13]

Art is little different from modern films and literature. "Modern art," said Finley Eversole, "with its loss of God and the human image, is the drama of our age. Here we see what really is happening to man, to society, and to man's faith in God."[14]

H. R. Rookmaaker, in his work *Modern Art and the Death of a Culture*, said:

> Modern art is not neutral . . . to look at modern art is to look at the fruit of the spirit of the avant-garde: it is they who are ahead in building a view of the world with no God, no norms.[15]

Lennon was involved as an artist within New York City's avant-garde movement. His works, some of which are reproduced in his two books *In His Own Write* and *A Spaniard in the Works*, have been described as

> replete with a cast of characters possessing real and a supernumerary genitals, imaginary and sometimes menacing animals. Like Picasso's lithographs, all but the essential was eliminated. There was often no background, no setting for the rational mind to focus on. The drawings were dreams, illusions—sometimes even nightmares—evoked on paper. This same inventiveness was apparent in many of the lyrics he wrote.[16]

In California, a recent college graduate told me about her experience in a university art class. Having noticed that she received *Cs* despite the superiority of her work to that of others who received *As*, she finally caught on. For her final project, she placed a piece of plywood on the freeway and then tossed paint as automobiles ran over the wood. It was her only *A* of the semester!

The absurdity in modern art is exemplified by the work of Walter DeMaria as reported in *Art in America*. DeMaria brought his art to New York in 1978 for the first time since 1969. He filled two separate galleries, "one with 26 stainless steel circles and squares, *the other with dirt*." A 3600 square-foot art gallery was filled with 22 cubic yards of dirt "distributed evenly throughout."

Commenting on the 220,000 pounds of dirt, an art critic said, "Even though DeMaria's ultimate goal seems to be the cool, elegant mental jamming, his art is not something you just think about. He is Duchampion with an ambitious '60 style added."[17] Marcel Duchamp,

Lennon's hero and one of the most influential men of our century, followed Picasso's lead by reflecting the world view that all life is absurd.

The Dada movement in 1917 portrayed the meaninglessness of traditional Western thought, art, morals, traditions. Its spirit was one of anarchy and nihilism, seeking authentic reality through absurdity. Irrationality and chance were its guides; even the movement's name was chosen at random by placing a finger in a French dictionary (*dada* is French for rocking chair). Observed Rookmaaker, "The wind is still blowing, and is becoming a storm, a storm called revolution."[18]

Surrealism, Dada's firstborn, also portrayed a negative view of life. The artists were against God, reason, nation, personality, conscience, beauty, talent, artistry; their work abounded with overt and concealed erotic symbolism.

Surrealism's spiritual leaders were the Marquis de Sade, Sigmund Freud, Friedrich Nietzsche, and Karl Marx. Pablo Picasso was its hero. John Lennon was its victim.

Surrealism had a far-reaching effect on him, Lennon said, "because then I realized that my imagery and my mind wasn't insanity; that if it was insane, I belonged in an exclusive club that sees the world in those terms. Surrealism to me is reality."[19] What Lennon failed to say in this interview, but did say elsewhere, was that his psychic visions of so-called reality were the result of taking LSD and other drugs.

Picasso once remarked, "Art is not to decorate apartments. Art is a weapon of revolution and my art is revolutionary art."[20] Once the revolution is accomplished, however, such revolutionary art is no longer permitted. Although Picasso was regarded as a hero in Russia, his art is no longer permitted there. His art is a weapon to destroy traditional values and concepts in nations influenced by Christianity.

Sir Herbert Read, a British Marxist and art critic, put it like this:

Everywhere the greatest obstacle to the creation of the new social reality is the cultural heritage of the past— the religion, the philosophy, the literature and the art which makes up the whole complex ideology of the bourgeois mind.[21]

One of America's greatest sculptors, Wheeler Williams, acknowledged that the purpose of modern art "was to destroy man's faith in his cultural heritage."[22]

Joan Bellaire, in an article entitled "Our Future as Revealed by Modern Art," maintained that art is a barometer of culture and that the twentieth century is dominated by an art characterized by its atheistic revolt against Christianity. She cited as examples the four atheists comprising the 1912 "Blue Riders"—Paul Klee, Lionel Feininger, Wassily Kandinsky, Alexia Jawlensky—two of whom, Kandinsky and Jawlensky, also were Marxists. She said, "The atheistic modern art has been able to assume control of almost all museums, art associations, and elementary, secondary, and college institutions of learning."[23]

Writing in the same vein, art critic Hans Sedlmayr claimed that the art of this century marks the *first atheistic century in modern history*. The nihilism and anarchism of artists who no longer believe in God pervade their work with characteristics which Sedlmayr labeled "demonic."[24]

Unfortunately, as Rookmaaker noted, "Christians have only too frequently not understood that art and literature, philosophy and even popular music were the agents of the new spirit of the age." He continued,

A new music emerged, again completely nonintellectual, with a thumping rhythm and shouting voices, each line and each beat full of the angry insult to all western values . . . their protest is in their music itself as well as in the words, for anyone who thinks that this is all cheap and no more than entertainment has never used his ears.[25]

Francis A. Schaeffer made this same point in *How Should We Then Live?* In chapter 10, "Modern Art, Music, Literature and Films," Schaeffer directly addressed the issue by stating that the expressed philosophy of art, music and literature "fits the world view being presented."[26] Indeed, art, music, and literature "expressed a world view and became a vehicle for carrying that world view to masses of people which the bare philosophic writings never would have touched."[27]

The philosophic writings, however, were important and in fact gave birth to the modern conscience. Thinkers spoke, artists painted, writers propagated, and musicians gave it the sound. Moreover, the philosophic writings were grounded in the atheism of Nietzsche, Darwin, Freud, Marx; atheistic artists were their offspring. In fact, the atheist Picasso is given credit for introducing the period of modern art in 1906–7 with his *Les Demoiselles d'Avignon*.

"It is worth reemphasizing," said Schaeffer, "that fragmentation in music is parallel to the fragmentation which occurred in painting."[28] "The music which came out of the biblical teaching of the Reformation," he said, "was shaped by that world view, so the world view of modern man shapes modern music."[29] What kind of music reflects this revolt against God? Said Schaeffer, "Popular music, such as the elements of rock, brought to the young people of the entire world the concept of a fragmented [i.e., atheistic] world."[30]

In other words, the world view emanating from Nietzsche, Freud, Darwin, and Marx was continued through Picasso, Kandinsky, and Pollock. It finally was unleashed to the masses through rock 'n' roll. No piece better illustrates this than John Lennon's famous "Imagine." It musically capsules modern secularism.

"Imagine there's no heaven," says Lennon, no hell, only a bit of sky with everyone living in the present. He moves on to no countries, no religion, no possessions . . . a place where the world will be united in every way.

By listening carefully to Lennon's utopia, we can understand why Mick Jagger of the Rolling Stones got away with his "Street Fighting Man." The song rings out with the declaration, "The time is right for violent revolution."

In a similar vein, we have Elton John's "Burn Down the Mission," which advocates burning down the rich man's house.

In contradiction to their sung ideology Elton John, Jagger, or Lennon bank millions of dollars every year.

In 1980, Malcolm Muggeridge wrote:

In the cycle of a great civilization, the artist begins as a priest and ends as a clown or buffoon. Examples of buffoonery in twentieth-century art, literature, and music are many: Dali, Picasso, John Cage, Beckett.[31]

He could well have listed John Lennon. Earlier he did speak to Lennon, his legacy, and his misled followers:

Our barbarians are home products indoctrinated at the public expense, urged on by the media systematically stage by stage, dismantling Christendom, depreciating and deprecating all its values. The whole social structure is now tumbling down, dethroning its God, undermining all its certainties. All this, wonderfully enough, is being done in the name of the health, wealth, and happiness of all mankind.[32]

We cannot close our eyes to rock music as a medium for atheism and despair. Rock music is evil because it is to music what Dada and surrealism are to art—atheistic, chaotic, nihilistic. Modern music, films, literature, and art reflect declared war against Christianity, whose weapons are messages of meaninglessness, immorality, anarchy, absurdity, and helplessness. A cultural matrix has been created which works to discredit the qualities necessary for the survival of civilized society.

Four

The Warfare

The Beatles legitimized rock 'n' roll and turned on the whole world. Their music and message appealed to all levels; their audiences were the largest ever enjoyed by any entertainers.

The Beatles set the trends, and their fans followed their lead. They were the vanguard of an entire generation who grew long hair, smoked grass, snorted coke, dropped acid, and lived for rock 'n' roll. They were the "cool" generation.

John Lennon and the Beatles invaded the United States in 1964 as a conquering army. The *Saturday Evening Post* warned us what to expect:

> To British intellectuals the Beatles are carrying the banner of the British beat generation, and their success represents a breakthrough for the *social rebellion* the Beatles represent (italics added).[1]

Most Americans were misled for we naively believed that four musicians equaled music. But the *Post* made it clear that there was much more to the package—*social rebellion.*

Quoting the Beatles' press officer, Derek Taylor said:

> It's incredible, absolutely incredible. Here are these four boys from Liverpool. They're *rude,* they're *pro-*

fane, they're *vulgar,* and they've taken over the world. It's as if they had founded a new religion. They're completely anti-Christ. I mean I am anti-Christ as well, but they're so anti-Christ, they shock me, which isn't an easy thing to do.[2]

Rudeness, profanity, vulgarity. Anti-Christ. These are not the finer, higher, purer qualities of Western civilization. But we must remember, the Beatles weren't representing Western civilization—they were advocating rebellion against its institutions!

This rebellion, not always apparent, is against Christianity and Christian moral values. But Lennon did not hide his antagonism toward Christianity. He said, "I was trying to say something or other about Christianity which I was opposed to at the time."[3]

Christianity had to be discredited in order to establish Lennon's atheistic, socialistic, hedonistic society. *If we fail to grasp this basic point, we cannot fully appreciate the dread influence of John Lennon and the Beatles.* Beatle George Harrison, for example, financed Monty Python's *Life of Brian,*[4] a film which *Newsweek* described as "one of the most irreverent."[5] *Time* commented:

> This is an excellent example of the movie's contempt for both taste and religion. *Life of Brian* is even now being protested by spokesmen for various pious groups. They are quite right to do so, for this is not gentle spoof, not good-natured satire of cherished beliefs. The Pythons assault on religion is . . . intense.[6]

Beatle Ringo Starr's favorite film directors are Frank Zappa and Ken Russell. According to *Rolling Stone,* "Ringo worked with Ken Russell on *Lisztomania* (1975), which featured The Who's Roger Daltrey as an oversexed Franz Liszt and Ringo as an anachronistically pop pope."[7]

In the film *Lisztomania,* according to *Time,* "Liszt disappears in the [deleted] of a paramour; later he sprouts a 10-foot phallus."[8] The Warner Brothers film was graphically advertised with porno posters portraying the male sex organ in volcanic activity.

Ken Russell's assault on morality and Christianity, however, is deep seated. Before *Lisztomania* he directed the counter-culture opera *Tommy,* and before *Tommy* he wrote and directed *The Devils* (starring Vanessa Redgrave), which depicted depraved nuns and priests performing lewd sex acts.

Tommy starred The Who rock group along with Elton John and Eric Clapton. Clapton was the movie's preacher who led a procession at a miracle-cure shrine where Marilyn Monroe was worshiped.

"*Tommy* is revolting and revolutionary to its cancerous core," said Anthony Hilder.

> It is without doubt and without exception the most blatantly anti-Christian movie malignancy ever made, at any time, anywhere, by any one. Its specific aim, like one of its songs, is to 'Rip Your Soul Apart.' It is distributed by Columbia Pictures on the Planet Earth, and in Hell by the Devil himself. . . . Everything is done to desecrate Christianity with all the lauding language of Lucifer.[9]

More recently, in 1980, Russell directed *Altered States,* another attack on Christianity. The Bible's account of creation, Christ, and the Cross are portrayed as myth. Evolution is portrayed as fact. The reality *Altered States* promises in place of the meaningful

Christian universe is "a hideous beginning, a meaningless existence, and a terrible end."[10]

Now we can better understand Paul McCartney's remark in early 1965, "We probably seem to be antireligious because of the fact that none of us believe in God."[11]

At the time, John Lennon tried to defuse the statement by saying that the Beatles were more agnostic than atheistic. He later was more straightforward regarding atheism. He accepted Hugh Schonfeld's thesis in *The Passover Plot* and regarded the scriptural account of Jesus' resurrection as a hoax.[12]

In *A Spaniard in the Works* (republished by the New American Library and promoted in the May 1981 *Book-of-the-Month Club News*), Lennon actually portrayed Jesus Christ guised as a jerk named Jesus El Pifco. Jesus is described as a "garlic eating, stinking, little, yellow, greasy fascist bastard Catholic Spaniard."[13]

This assault on the virgin birth of Christ should have put Lennon on the outside looking in, but, mystery of mysteries, it only endeared him to his vast following of believers and unbelievers. Elsewhere in his irreverent tome he wrote, "Whistling a quaint Spanish refrain Jesus was dreaming of his loved wombs back home in their little white fascist huts."[14]

One chapter actually contained the following dialogue: " 'Hello, you Rev boy.' 'Well Mr. Wabooba, may I call you Wog? What is the basic problem you are facing?' 'You white trash Christian boy.' " Instead of Father, Son, and Holy Spirit, Lennon blasphemed with "Fahter, Sock, and Mickey Most." Instead of God, it's "Griff." "In Griff's eye, we are all a bunch of bananas, swinging in the breeze—waiting as it were Wabooba to be peeled."[15]

To Lennon, we were a bunch of bananas swaying in the breeze. Today, according to Pink Floyd, we are merely bricks in a wall. Talk about a spiritual wasteland! No direction. No sense. Instead of offering hopes, plans, and dreams, the rock culture offers drugs and sex, sex and drugs.

After reviewing Lennon's missive of nihilism, *Parade Magazine* said:

> Parents who believe the Beatles are a quartet of fine, wholesome, uplifting musicians who hold young womanhood in high light and respect, might do well to peruse Lennon's second work for insight into at least one literate Beatle's morality and mentality.[16]

Lennon and the Beatles were discharging their obligations to rebellion. Once we understand this and recall Lennon's statement that the Beatles did nothing without considering its consequences, many disjointed pieces of a controversial puzzle fall into place, including Lennon's bombshell:

> Christianity will go. It will vanish and shrink. I needn't argue about that; I'm right and I will be proven right. We're more popular than Jesus now.[17]

This was no off-the-cuff statement. Only when Lennon realized his personal beliefs might financially jeopardize the Beatles' tour in the United States did he offer a "slight retraction." But even then Hunter Davies ironically reported that the Beatles' concerts in the Bible-belt South "were the best of all."[18]

In reality the Beatles had little cause for concern since they enjoyed media protection from bad publicity.

Besides, misled teenagers by the millions were simultaneously wearing both "I love Jesus" and "I love the Beatles" lapel buttons.

For "four iconoclastic, brass-hard, post-Christian, pragmatic realists,"[19] (as Paul McCartney described them) the Beatles in general—and John Lennon in particular—were idolized around the world. Hedonism, atheism, and blasphemy were lucrative pursuits.

Lennon's atheism reached maturity in "God" (the Plastic Ono Band album, 1970), and in his most famous song, "Imagine," written in 1971. Lennon assured his followers, "There ain't no Jesus gonna come from the sky" in "I Found Out," although he lamented "now that I found out I know I can cry." He made it clear he has seen through religion "from Jesus to Paul" as he equated religion with drugs. In fact, Lennon warned against religion *and* drugs—"don't let them fool you with dope and cocaine."

Before his death, Lennon admitted the Beatles used a great deal of cocaine in their day, "but it's a dumb drug."[20]

But Lennon admitted smoking marijuana now and then, and using hallucinogenic mushrooms or peyote.

"God" and "Imagine" summarily state Lennon's atheistic philosophy. As one Beatle spokesman said, "And there was 'God' where John threw off the yokes and made a stand."[21]

"The dream is over," said Lennon. God is merely a concept "by which we measure our pain." To him, God was not a reality, only a concept—rather clever philosophical atheism for one who never trusted "intellectuals."

Lennon said in song that he didn't believe in the

Bible, Jesus, magic, Buddha, yoga, or even the Beatles. Instead, he said, "I just believe in me / Yoko and me / And that's reality."[22]

In closing "God," he instructed his millions of listeners, "and so dear friends, you just have to carry on, the dream is over." God does not exist! Lennon didn't cry. Lennon, the dreamweaver, then knew better.

But "Imagine" is much more profound. "If I had to pick one song that represented the finest aspects of John Lennon," said *Rolling Stone* magazine, "I'd choose 'Imagine.'"[23]

Ironically, even though Lennon was never a Christian pilgrim, *Rolling Stone* also reported the following:

> At a Christmas Eve mass at New York's Cathedral of St. John the Divine—the world's largest church—Paul Moore, Jr., the bishop of New York, lauded John Lennon as "a man of peace." Following the benediction, the church's pipe organ solemnly sounded the strains of "Imagine."[24]

"Imagine," as mentioned earlier, is so written that it nearly summarizes in one song the secularist's dream. Both the Marxist and the humanist are well pleased with "Imagine" because it postulates neither heaven nor hell. The secularist likes that idea because everyone is living "for today." The modernist certainly likes that idea, too. "There are no countries" since the goal is "a brotherhood of man" in which "the world will be as one"—again, the quest of all who believe in one world government.

We also are told that there is to be no religion (since God never existed), no possessions, only socialism. "All the people sharing all the world."

Lennon's world view is poetic and powerful—atheism, socialism, a world state; no God, no nations, no capitalistic warmongers; a free society where people do their own thing; rock 'n' roll music, drugs, plenty of sex; a hedonistic paradise.

In Lennon's "Well Well Well" he talks of revolution, women's liberation, and so on.

Yoko Ono's "Approximately Infinite Universe" (1973) delivered a strong women's liberation message with lines such as "if you keep hammering anti-abortion, we'll tell you no more [expletive deleted] for men."

Lennon's world view was implemented on this earth. God wasn't invited, but drugs, sex and rock'n' roll were! Hedonism abounded. Youth was there in abundance. Energy was everywhere. "Happiness, energy, lucidity and fantasy could all be obtained by the selection of the right kind of dope."[25]

December 6, 1969, Lennon's utopian society was realized at the Altamont Rolling Stones rock concert in California.

An eye witness recounted the rock 'n' roll concert which contained everything Lennon asked for in "God," "Well Well Well," "I Found Out," and "Imagine."

"By midday virtually everyone was tripping."[26] This made the rock crowd happy, and besides, "Happiness is a Warm Gun" (if "Happiness" isn't a drug song, replace it with Lennon's "Day Tripper," which Lennon admitted is).

"The festival of love was becoming a catechism, and nobody could control it. A man was almost killed as he tried to fly from a speedway bridge—another acid case."[27]

"Fights broke out everywhere."[28]

"I could see a guy from the stage who had a knife and just wanted to stab somebody."

"Kids were being stabbed and heads cracked the whole time."

Four people were brutally murdered that day by the Hell's Angels, and hundreds, perhaps thousands, were wounded.

"On this day hip jargon, flower power, and the Age of Aquarius were finished,"[29] said Sanchez.

> It was here that the utopian myth of the 'Hair-Oz-Stones generation was ripped aside to expose the lie beneath. The anarchy these kids espoused *worked only with the backup of the straight society they despised* . . . this was the permissive society . . . the freedom for all . . . It was ugly, mindless, blind, black and terrifying.[30]

Lennon's imagined society was supposed to have been a dream, but the reality at Altamont was a nightmare. Although Lennon is hailed as a "man of peace," his philosophy is a working formula for murderous anarchy.

The Beatle tours also were somewhat miniature portraits of Lennon's new society.

The Beatles experimented with the commandments on one hand, and they laid the foundation for drugs on the other.

Ringo reported that the only fun part of touring was the hotel in the evening, with the pot and the girls. "We got drunk a lot. You couldn't help it. We had a lot of girls. We soon realized that they were easy to get."[31]

In 1964 *all four Beatles could have been arrested for statutory rape.*[32]

The Beatles exploitation of vulnerable teenage girls is

a matter of public record, but we need only quote John Lennon's own words. Lennon downrates Hunter Davies' book *The Beatles* because "there was nothing about the orgies." Lennon said:

> Beatles tours were like the Fellini film *Satyricon*. We had the image. Man, our tours were like something else. They were Satyricon, all right. Derek's and Neil's rooms were always full of junk. When we hit a town, we hit it. There's photographs of me crawling about in Amsterdam on my knees coming out of [deleted] houses and things like that.[33]

It should be noted that when he indulged in this sort of behavior, Lennon was still married to Cynthia, his first wife and the mother of his son. In fact, he did *The Two Virgins* album (an album whose cover consisted of Lennon and Yoko Ono nude both front and back) with Yoko while married to Cynthia. His attitude toward extra-marital activity was that

> intellectually, we knew marriage was a stupid scene, but we're romantic and square as well as hip and aware. We lived together for a year before we got married, but we were still tied to other people by a bit of paper.[34]

Of course, when Lennon and Ono broke up for a spell, Lennon reverted to his old ways:

> May Pang, 30, who worked for Apple, the Beatles' recording company, later became personal secretary to John Lennon and his wife, Yoko Ono. When Yoko and John split in 1973, Lennon took off with May Pang, spent six months with her in Los Angeles, another 12 in Manhattan. It was 'true love' on May's part, but Lennon's infatuation was largely sexual.[35]

Instead of using his musical brilliance for good, Lennon chose evil. Those deifying him need to seriously consider what it is they feel worth canonizing. His atheism? His gross immorality? His drugs? His social rebellion? His world view? If we could answer this question, we could also discover why Western civilization is crumbling. Jenkin Lloyd Jones once took a quick look at the rock 'n' roll scene and wrote, "Great civilizations and animal standards of behavior coexist only for short periods."[36]

Anthropologist J. D. Unwin took a longer look and concluded, "Any human society is free to choose either to display great energy or to enjoy sexual freedom. The evidence is that it cannot do both for more than one generation."[37]

Five

The Pusher

Since John Lennon's death, more Beatle records and albums and songs are being sold than ever before. *The Beatles/1967–1970*, produced by Capitol Records, leads off with "Strawberry Fields Forever." Indeed, eight of the first eleven songs concern drugs, and they're followed by "Back in the USSR" and the irreverent "Ballad of John and Yoko."

Capitol's latest edition of *The Beatles Yesterday and Today* contains the drug song "Day Tripper." *The Beatles Rarities*, apart from its sadistic inside picture, contains "I Am the Walrus" and "Penny Lane."

Our present generation is saturated with drugs—16 million marijuana users and five hundred thousand heroin addicts. It doesn't seem possible that we could tolerate such a situation. Yet we not only tolerate it, we encourage it. Drug songs are played every single day over radio airwaves and on millions of stereos.

"When the Beatles did get into drugs," said a recent pro-Beatles publication, "they smoked grass and dropped acid with the same enthusiasm they brought to everything."[1] And because they did, millions of impressionable youth followed the Pied Pipers of Liverpool.

The Beatles had the word, they were giving out the

word, the kids were picking up the word, and the word was drugs.

"The rock scene is permeated by the values and practices of the drug culture," said a pamphlet published in 1979 by the U.S. Department of Health, Education, and Welfare. "Many rock stars have become cult heroes and many of them take drugs."[2]

The pamphlet further stated:

Children can often identify the current rock stars, and many identify with their life styles. When popular musicians are arrested for drug possession, some of the popular media—especially the rock music radio stations—portray them sympathetically and mock the enforcers of the drug laws.[3]

Although we discussed the situation in *The Marxist Minstrels*,[4] the authoritative *U.N. Bulletin on Narcotics* presents a more convincing analysis.

In an article entitled "Approbation of Drug Usage in Rock and Roll Music," author S. Taqi said that after *Sgt. Pepper's*, drug usage themes in rock 'n' roll visibly increased. Moreover, there was progressively less outcry against them. The *Pepper* album gave the green light to drugs as "in" songwriter's material.

Taqi noted that drug usage "is a very real part of the rock and roll world" and that many artists believe the pro-drug lyrics of their songs; that is, they believe that drugs induce a meaningful and valuable experience.

Taqi said that after one or two record companies went on the line with drug-centered materials, "the rest of the [rock 'n' roll] industry had to follow or be left out in the cold. The larger companies were plagued by the fact that if they did not get on the bandwagon with 'underground' materials, the dozens of smaller companies with no such pangs of conscience would snatch a large percentage of sales away from them."

The author's conclusion is sobering. He said, "the end result is that when an urban child, who lives in the ordinary world, is offered a marijuana cigarette or a dose of LSD, he will remember them not as something his health and hygiene teacher spoke warningly about, but as something Mick Jagger, or John Lennon, or Paul McCartney has used and enjoyed."[5]

There is no doubt the Beatles and rock musicians set the stage for drugs. Their followers did the rest. "It was the mid-sixties and everyone was smoking grass," said Steve Stone in a magazine article written in praise of Lennon.

> Rock groups seemed to be expanding their consciousness as well as their bank books with songs about drugs. Certain groups seemed to exude the smell of marijuana—The Grateful Dead, The Jefferson Airplane, Big Brother, The Rolling Stones.[6]

Now it is the eighties and everyone is still smoking grass! In fact, more people are smoking it now than ever before. Rock groups are still "expanding their consciousness" with dope. The drug-pushing albums of the mid-sixties are still being sold to our youth. Music is functioning as a hooker for drugs!

A decade ago jazz critic Gene Lees warned us to be careful. Unfortunately, few listened. Said Lees,

> About three years ago, having caught the reference to drugs—indeed, the exhortation of their use—buried in a lot of rock and folk-rock lyrics, I wrote an article, suggesting that if this continued, the country was in for a wave of drug use that could shake its foundations. . . . Rock music has widened the inevitable and normal gap

between generations, turned it from something healthy—and absolutely necessary to forward movement—into something negative, destructive, nihilistic.[7]

To better understand our present plight, however, we need to go back and pick up at least the following bits and pieces.

In a *Rolling Stone* interview, John Lennon admitted he began taking LSD in 1964. "How long did it go?" he was asked. "It went on for years" he replied. "I must of had a thousand trips . . . a thousand. I used to just eat it all the time."[8]

When the *Rolling Stone* interviewer said, "There's a lot of obvious LSD things you did in the music," Lennon replied, "Yes."[9]

In an interview given shortly before his death, Lennon said the Beatles were smoking marijuana for breakfast and nobody could communicate with them because they were "just all glazed eyes."[10]

Although Lennon conceded that the Beatles turned on to pot in 1965[11] ("Help" and "Rubber Soul" were drug oriented, he said), and that "Day Tripper" in 1966 was a drug song,[12] (as was "Yellow Submarine"), it wasn't until 1967's *Sgt. Pepper's Lonely Hearts Club Band* that the barriers came tumbling down.

Sgt. Pepper's heralded the drug revolution in this country, a revolution still unchecked. *There is no guarantee we'll survive it.*

Max Rafferty once said that rock music and drugs go together like Mary and Mary's little lamb. Millions of parents could testify that their son or daughter, hooked on rock music and worshiping its stars, fell into the drug culture. Thousands also could testify that rock and drugs were precipators of tragic accidents, even suicide.

Lest we think that such a situation is easy to correct, consider the following from the *Chicago Tribune:*

> Outraged by the Jefferson Airplane song, "White Rabbit," because of its drug lyrics, the Nixon administration ordered the FCC to ban all songs with such lyrics, but public outcry was immediate and the ban was hastily lifted.[13]

Yet as mentioned earlier, Congressman Lester Wolff (D-N.Y.) acknowledged,

> Drug abuse among our children has risen in the past two years from epidemic to pandemic proportions. It has grown so large that neither the nation—nor any nation in history—has ever before faced a problem that is so insidious and so dangerous. And if we don't recognize the importance of this problem, it will have disastrous effects upon our society.[14]

Must we be so helpless as a nation? Andrew Fletcher wrote in 1704:

> I know a very wise man who believed that if a man were permitted to make all the ballads, he need not care who should make the laws of a nation. And we find that most of the ancient legislators thought they could not well reform the manners of any city without the help of a lyric and sometimes of a dramatic poet.[15]

Time magazine reported that the *Sgt. Pepper's* album was "drenched in drugs,"[16] and Hunter Davies acknowledged in *The Beatles* that the one album which "showed many traces of their interest in drugs" was the *Sgt. Pepper's* album.[17] *Time* further stated that the Beatles' flirtation with drugs and their drop-out attitude expressed in songs like "A Day in the Life" (removed from BBC because of its drug implications[18]) disturbs many fans and worried parents.

In the *Sgt. Pepper's* album, Ringo Starr quiveringly said "I get high with a little help from my friends." According to *Time,* "Lucy in the Sky with Diamonds" invokes a drug-induced hallucination, and even the initials of the primary words in the title spell out LSD, though the Beatles plead innocence. "Lucy in the Sky with Diamonds," however, was advertised on posters with the letters LSD underlined, and is listed in the drug column of Dave Marsh and Kevin Stein's work *The Book of Rock Lists* published by Dell and Rolling Stone Press.

Time further said that the overall drug theme is no coincidence since all four Beatles admitted taking LSD occasionally. "The fact remains that when the Beatles talk—about drugs, the war in Vietnam, religion—millions listen, and this is the new situation in the pop music world."[19]

The drug culture was given a booster shot when RSO Records reissued *Sgt. Pepper's* in 1978. The new album consisted of twenty-eight songs—nearly one-half drug related! The Bee Gees sing "A Day in the Life" and "With a Little Help From My Friends." George Burns sings "Fixing a Hole," and Sandy Farina does "Strawberry Fields Forever." Peter Frampton, Aerosmith, Alice Cooper (of "I Love the Dead" fame), Earth Wind and Fire, Steve Martin, Paul Nicholas and Billy Preston all contributed to this outrageous disc. The record has since been made into a full-length motion picture.

This travesty was augmented by *Newsweek's* glowing seven-page review. *Newsweek* even mentions LSD guru Dr. Timothy Leary as favoring the record and film.[20] But *Newsweek* didn't mention Leary's dismissal from professorship at Harvard University because he led his students into drugs. Harvard didn't approve of Leary's introducing his students to drugs. We don't approve of rock 'n' roll's doing so either. And we don't approve of *Newsweek's* encouraging *Sgt. Pepper's*!

Compounding the issue is the fact that the performers were aware of *Sgt. Pepper's* drug theme. The Bee Gees certainly knew. They admitted openly, "We do smoke marijuana now and again."[21] Alice Cooper is no fool. George Burns may not have known, but RSO certainly did. *Newsweek* is usually perceptive in regard to these issues.

The irony of it! Teenagers listen to this music every day, even during lunch breaks in school. And we're wondering why we're experiencing a drug epidemic! Some high schools sponsor a state trooper for one hour once a year to warn students against drugs—yet these same students feed daily on a diet of "I Get High with a Little Help from My Friends."

"Drug taking is nothing new to the music business," said one industry spokesman, "but it has always been a secretive thing. No one went around boasting about it, but now it is really getting out of hand."[22] The music reviewer for *Holiday* magazine concurred. He questioned, "Is it possible that the record producers have been fooled by the jargon of the song—have put out such discs not knowing what they mean?"

> It is unlikely because it is impossible to be in the music business long without seeing pot smoked. The terminology of narcotics is widely known and understood in the industry, both by artists, recorder, and producer. . . . In songs meant for children of twelve and even younger, they proclaim that it is wise, hip, and inside to dissolve your responsibilities and problems of a difficult world into the mists of marijuana, LSD, or heroin.[23]

Those inside the music industry know the advantages of dealing in pot. Rock groups, in general, have few or no qualms about using drugs. Said *Time* magazine,

> Rock musicians use drugs frequently and openly, and their compositions are riddled with references to drugs, from the Beatles' "I Get High With A Little Help From My Friends" to the Jefferson Airplane's "White Rabbit". . . .[24]

Cavalier claimed that "handfuls of rock groups have been liberated by acid [LSD]."[25] Grace Slick, a former lead singer with The Jefferson Airplane, told *Cavalier:*

> We all use drugs and we condone the judicious use of drugs by everyone. Kids are going to blow their minds somehow, and this is a better way to do it than racking up their car against the wall. Let them groove, do their thing, ball on the grass in the open. I dig watching people make love.[26]

Frank Zappa of the Mothers of Invention told *Life* that society's major hang-ups could be cured by drugs and sexual openness.[27] Dr. Hook's *Sloppy Seconds,* cut by Columbia Records, reeked with similar sentiments.[28]

According to *High Times* magazine which advertises itself as a magazine which stands for "dope, sex and rock 'n' roll":

> LSD made its debut in rock in 1962 in a single by the Gamblers. By 1965, Eric Burden and The Animals were crooning their love song, "To Sandoz" (the discoverer of LSD). The Rolling Stones were singing about how "Something Happened to Me Yesterday," The Byrds were harmonizing about how they were "Eight Miles High," and The Beatles had long been advising everyone to "Turn off your mind, relax, and float downstream. . . . This is not dying?"[29]

Grace Slick admitted, "It's hard to keep an eye on the kid while you're hallucinating."[30] And *TV Guide* acknowledged that "the average rock musician likes to perform [in an environment] of stomping, cheering crowds, typically well-dosed with alcohol and marijuana."[31]

One of the verses in Lou Reed's *Street Hassle* advised a fellow junkie how to dispose of his overdosed girl friend. Just put her in the street, he said, "and by morning she's just another hit and run."

Parade magazine discussed the relationship between rock stars and drugs:

> We know that Elvis Presley, the greatest rock 'n' roller of his time, was a drug-bedeviled addict. We know that Paul McCartney, 37 . . . is a user of marijuana. . . . We know that guitarist Keith Richards of the Rolling Stones and his common-law wife, Anita Pallenberg, used to shoot heroin. We know that punk rock musician Sid Vicious stabbed his sweetheart to death, then "mainlined" his own life away via heroin. We know that Greg Allman, Mick Jagger, the late Jimi Hendrix and Janis Joplin . . . all the rock stars on pot, cocaine, heroin, uppers, downers, and in-betweeners. . . .[32]

The University of Wisconsin student newspaper, *The Daily Cardinal,* stated that the Beatles have "proselytized the use of drugs so subtly that words and conceptions once only common to drug users are found in sentences of teeny-boppers and statesmen alike."[33]

In Hunter Davies' authorized biography of the Beatles, readers are informed that the Beatles "have used drug slang in their songs."[34] Davies' only comment was that he found it strange that several deliberate slang obsenities went unnoticed.

In an article entitled "The New Far-Out Beatles," *Life* magazine quoted Paul McCartney to the effect that LSD was a universal cure-all. McCartney said:

> After I took it, it opened my eyes. We only use 1/10 of our brain. Just think what we could accomplish if we could only tap that hidden part! It could mean a whole new world. If politicians would take LSD, there wouldn't be any more war or poverty or famine.[35]

In the Beatles' biography, Jane Asher acknowledged that McCartney was on LSD; in fact the house "was full of the stuff." Paul himself agreed, although he insisted he was the last of the four to try pot and LSD.[36]

According to the official records, the Beatles' introduction to drugs began in Hamburg, Germany, where they bandied vulgarisms, shouted "Nazis" in English and told the Germans "to [deleted] off."[37] Lennon said, "We learned from the Germans that you could stay awake by eating slimming pills, so we did that." Although the pills were supposed to be fairly harmless, the Beatles progressed to the more potent Black Bombers and Purple Hearts.[38]

By July 1967, the Beatles, throwing caution to the wind, signed a full-page advertisement in the *London Times* calling for the legalization of marijuana in Britain.[39]

Influenced by marijuana, not only *Sgt. Pepper's* but also *Magical Mystery Tour* was pressed. Davies reported that the Beatles arrived at the EMI Studios at 7:30 one evening to record *Magical Mystery Tour* but had only the title and a few bars of the music. Paul played the opening bars on the piano, showing the others how it would go. Davies said that Paul gestured a lot with his hands and shouted flash, flash, flash, saying it would be like a commercial . . . [John] opened the sporran and took out some pot, which he lit, then passed it around. They all had a drag.[40]

From marijuana, the four turned to LSD. Lennon frankly stated that LSD was the drug that really pointed the way. He said, "I was suddenly struck by great visions when I first took acid. But you have got to be looking for it before you possibly find it."[41] Davies noted that it was through drugs that they discovered themselves.[42] He reported that their most creative year was 1967—"the year of LSD, and Maharishi."[43] It was also the year of *Sgt. Pepper's*.

In November, 1968, John Lennon was convicted for the possession of marijuana and fined $360. Scotland Yard's dogs sniffed out the drug when they raided the apartment of John and his Japanese mistress. Inspectors found traces of marijuana in a cigarette rolling machine and in an empty film tin. They found 219 grams in an envelope and in a binocular case. This conviction nearly cost Lennon the right to live in the United States, but under tremendous pressure the Immigration and Naturalization department relented. Lennon might have been better off had he been refused for Lennon's assassin, Mark David Chapman, probably would have stayed in Hawaii.

In April, 1969, a Scotland Yard dog found George Harrison and his wife, Patty, with enough pot for 120 cigarettes. Both pleaded guilty and were fined $600 apiece.[44]

In 1972 Paul McCartney, his wife, and Wings drummer Denny Seiwell were fined $1,800 after pleading guilty to smuggling six ounces of marijuana into Sweden. In 1973 McCartney was fined $240 after pleading guilty to growing marijuana plants on his Scottish Highland farm. In 1975 McCartney's wife, Linda, was arrested in Los Angeles for possession of marijuana, but the charges were later dropped. In 1980 McCartney was arrested in Tokyo for possession of marijuana.

In the Beatles' December, 1968, White album *The Beatles,* the song "Glass Onion" contained a reference to strawberry fields (alluding to "Strawberry Fields Forever" written during their "creative-drug-year-of-1967") and went on to say that, "here is another place . . . where everything flows." Lennon's "Cold Turkey," recorded in 1969, consisted of drug-based lyrics.

But it was Lennon who said, "If people can't face up to the fact of other people being naked or smoking pot, . . . then we're never going to get anywhere."[45]

The drug counter-culture of the Beatles unrelentingly has made progressive inroads. Lennon once emerged from his pad and told our youth to "turn off your mind, relax, and float downstream."

Commonweal charged that the Beatles' recordings abounded with drug implications.[46] And *Time* reported a Chicago college student who smoked marijuana regularly as having said, "You take it when you're going to see *Yellow Submarine.* It's not to solve problems, just to giggle."[47] *Cavalier* confessed that sound engineers are still trying to reproduce the *Sgt. Pepper's* effects for pot smoking.[48]

This is why Art Linkletter referred to the Beatles as the "leading missionaries of the acid society."[49] Testifying before the House Select Committee on Crime, Mr. Linkletter said that the Beatles, rock music, and Timothy Leary were strong contributors to the drug crisis facing America today. He said:

> Today in the top 40 pop records played by rock groups, I would say at least half of them are a constant secret message to the whole teenage world to drop out, to turn on, to groove with chemicals.[50]

Lennon's legacy continues to wreak havoc. Too few of our youth are informed enough to protest. Instead, one of the world's most influential pot pushers is regarded as an international hero. His drug music continues to be sounded over the airwaves.

While millions of families desperately try to rescue their children from the unspeakably evil clutches of the drug culture—a culture largely created and promoted by the rock 'n' roll industry—the industry entices these same children right back into it. If more parents catch on, woe be to the industry.

Six

The Radical

"Revolution was in the air," said Tony Sanchez in *Up and Down with the Rolling Stones* (published by Morrow in 1979).

This is a statement worth noting because discussions of revolution, Marxism, or socialism are frequently thought to be alarmist topics germinated solely in radical right fever swamps. Tony Sanchez is no radical rightist, yet he addressed and detailed the radicalism of Mick Jagger because Jagger's views are an important part of Rolling Stones history. Jagger viewed rock music as an instrument for social change.

Jagger's radicalism is significant because John Lennon claimed to be as radical as Jagger! Said Lennon, "I resent the implications that the Stones are like revolutionaries and that the Beatles weren't. If the Stones were or are, the Beatles really were, too."[1]

This is undoubtedly true. Sanchez told about a Beatles and Rolling Stones meeting where they talked "long into the night about music and revolution and Chuck Berry and how they were all going to change the world."[2]

Before tracing Lennon's "change the world" radicalism, however, it will help to understand Jagger's radicalism as perceived by one who spent years with the Rolling Stones.

According to Sanchez, Jagger's interest in revolution was kindled at the London School of Economics. It was decided there that the old, present order would be overthrown and replaced with a new, "freer" society.[3] The school's slogan in January, 1969, was straightforward: "Kill the Bourgeoisie."

The London School of Economics was established by the leftist Fabian Socialists of Great Britain under the leadership of Sidney Webb, whose monumental volume praising Joseph Stalin and the USSR, *Soviet Communism—A New Civilization*, later turned out to be written not by Webb, but by the Soviet Foreign Office.[4]

Jagger talked about Marx and Lenin, according to Sanchez. "Although he disagreed with their doctrines, he understood the fundamental wrongness of capitalism."[5]

Jagger became a "committed revolutionary,"[6] however, following his conviction and three-month sentence for possession of narcotics. Sanchez said:

> Mick wasn't playing at revolution anymore. I realized then that he genuinely wanted to see society overthrown, that he really felt a revolution coming and that he saw the Stones as the vanguard of a historical bloody period of change.[7]

"He leaped at the chance of joining the revolution," said Sanchez, "when tens of thousands of angry young people stormed into Grosvenor Square to demonstrate their hatred of American imperialism and the Vietnam war."[8]

"There should be no such thing as private property," said multimillionaire Mick Jagger. "Anybody should be able to go where he likes and do what he likes."[9]

To fan the flames of revolution, Jagger wrote "Street Fighting Man" which said in part, "Now is the time for violent revolution." The song was used during the 1968 Democratic National Convention in Chicago to stir the blood of the Students for a Democratic Society (SDS) and other radical groups who disrupted the convention.

"Street Fighting Man," along with "Sympathy for the Devil," were recorded on the Stones' *Beggar Banquet* album, a controversial album whose original jacket design called for a toilet, a roll of toilet paper, some select four-letter words on the wall, and the title "God Rolls His Own." Although Jagger did not find the cover idea offensive, Decca records did. The album was finally released in a plain white jacket.

Commenting on the album the *Yale Daily News* said:

> Rock music censors who banned the Rolling Stones' "Street Fighting Man" are going to have their hands full when they hear *Beggars Banquet,* the group's latest album. Six of the ten songs are blatantly revolutionary, their heavy rhythm pounding, mobilizing, appealing to the people . . . The Rolling Stones are definitely back in the revolutionary hard rock thing.[10]

Jagger's religious affections can best be understood with the following description of the Rolling Stones' concert at Altamont on December 6, 1969. Reported Sanchez:

> The more they [the spectators at this particular rock concert] were beaten and bloodied [by the Hell's Angels], the more they were impelled, as if by some supernatural force, to offer themselves as human sacrifices to these agents of Satan. The violence transcended all comprehension. It had become some primeval ritual. . . And now the pounding voodoo drumming and the primitive shrieks echoed out, and the Rolling Stones were into their song of homage to the Antichrist. . . . 'Sym-

pathy for the Devil' became the focus of all the evil energy roaring through the crowd.[11]

The social revolution preached by the Rolling Stones endeared them to the Marxist-Leninists who recognized the group's pro-Red leanings. One Communist newspaper printed in New York City remarked: "They may not be sure where their heads are, but their hearts are out in the streets."[12]

According to Ralph J. Gleason, when the Rolling Stones first came to the West Coast, a group of young radicals issued a statement of welcome. It read in part: "The revolutionary youth of the world hears your music and is inspired to even more deadly acts. . . . We will play your music . . . as we tattoo BURN BABY BURN on the bellies of the wardens and generals and create a new society from the ashes of our fires . . . you will play your splendid music . . . under the hanging corpses of priests, under a million red flags waving over a million anarchist communities . . . LONG LIVE THE REVOLUTION!"[13]

John Lennon and the Beatles were an integral part of this same revolutionary milieu and received high marks from the same Communist press—especially for the White album which contained "Back in the USSR" and "Piggies." One line from "Back in the USSR" nearly left the Marxists speechless: "You don't know how lucky you are boy . . . Back in the USSR."

The W. E. B. DuBois Clubs of America (said to have been spawned by the Communist Party USA, according to J. Edgar Hoover in the October 1964 *Law Enforcement Bulletin*) mentioned the Beatles in its first publication:

> The social consciousness of the Beatles has gotten little play in the American press, but it becomes evident to

the followers of the group who are tuned into such things.[14]

Lennon, like Jagger of the Rolling Stones, was a man of the revolution. He wrote for the revolution. He sang for the revolution. He donated money for the revolution. He, along with Paul McCartney, existentialist Jean Paul Sartre, and one hundred and twenty-five others signed a petition calling for the immediate American withdrawal from Vietnam.[15] The petition did not ask for Communist North Vietnam to withdraw its forces from South Vietnam.

"Working Class Hero" was, according to Lennon, "a song for the revolution."[16] "I hope," he said, "it's about what 'Give Peace a Chance' was about."[17] It was indeed! "Give Peace a Chance" was about America losing the war in Vietnam to the Communists. "Working Class Hero" is the communist who is fighting America. The two songs fit hand in glove.

Unexplainably, Lennon continues to be called a "man of peace," or a "fighter for peace," The Rt. Rev. Paul Moore, Jr., Bishop of New York, praised Lennon as a "man of peace."[18] The Soviet press mourned him as a "fighter for peace," one who took a public position "in opposition to the dirty initiatives of the American military."[19]

"Give Peace a Chance" was, in reality, a declaration of war against the United States. Lennon told *Newsweek*, "when you stop and think, what the . . . was I doing *fighting* the American government."[20] Lennon's revolutionary songs, marches, rallies, and contributions were all acts of war. He had already declared war on Christianity ("Jesus is a garlic eating stinking little yellow greasy Fascist bastard Catholic"); he had already declared war on biblical morality ("If we couldn't get groupies, we would have [deleted] and everything, whatever was going"[21]); he had already declared war on laws regulating drugs, especially marijuana.

Under the guise of peace and love, he sold revolution, lust, and decadence. *Two Virgins* sold revolution under the guise of love; "Give Peace a Chance" sold revolution under the guise of peace. Drugs and sex, love and peace. These techniques—a part of Lennon's legacy—are still at work on our youth.

"The battle lines involved much more than music," wrote Vern Stefanic. "The Lennon-led Beatles brought to the American youth culture—a new drug culture—political awareness, as conservative groups quickly identified the Beatles' music—and many of Lennon's views as communist. They considered him anti-God, anti-American, pro-drugs and pro-revolution. They asked, 'This is a hero?'"[22]

Lennon was indeed anti-religion ("God" and "Imagine"), anti-American ("Give Peace a Chance" and "Sometime in New York City"), pro-drugs ("Sgt. Pepper's," "Rubber Soul," "Cold Turkey") and pro-revolution ("Working Class Hero" and "Sometime in New York City").

"I wanted to put out what I felt about revolution," said Lennon. "I thought it was about time we spoke about it."[23] And speak he did. When *Rolling Stone* magazine mentioned that a violent revolution might be the end of the world, Lennon actually objected:

> Not necessarily, they say that every time, but I don't really believe it . . . I used to think I wish a earthquake or revolution would happen so I could go out and steal and do what the blacks are doing now.[24]

Lennon's "Revolution No. 9" was a subconscious audio track of how a revolution might sound. He then said, "I really thought that love would save us. But now I'm wearing a Chairman Mao badge, that's where it's at. I'm just beginning to think he's doing a good job."[25]

Besides "Working Class Hero," "Imagine," "God," "Back in the USSR" and "Piggies" (by George Harrison), Lennon was singing "Power to the People," "Angela," and "Give Peace a Chance." When he wasn't writing copy for the revolution, he was performing at so-called Peace Rallies which were invariably anti-American, anti-moral, pro-drug, pro-Communist rallies. The international socialist hive buzzed and Lennon was a very important worker bee!

"Call him a hero or call him a rebel," said rock critic Vern Stefanic, "in the late 1960s, his social views— admittedly Marxist in nature—dominated his life."[26] Stefanic could have mentioned the early '70s, too, since Lennon wrote "Working Class Hero" in 1970 along with "God." In 1971, he wrote his most accomplished revolutionary number, "Imagine," in which atheism, socialism, and world government were preached (exactly what Marx and Lenin had preached; exactly what Mick Jagger was preaching). *Sometime in New York City,* an album of revolution, was produced in 1972.

Lennon had been involved with social rebellion since he was seventeen years old. The sexual revolution, the drug culture, and his atheistic, anti-Christ philosophy were the weapons in his war against "oppressive" Western society.

Consider Lennon and Yoko Ono's *Two Virgins.* The album was created in sin. Lennon was married to another woman, yet the album cover showed John and his future wife Yoko nude both front and back side. Nudity was avant garde. Faithfulness, purity, and self-respect became old order virtues!

"The *Two Virgins* album was typical of the John Lennon/Yoko Ono style of innocent revolution," said one reporter. "On one hand, they were shaking up society, but on the other hand, they were doing it with the soft hands that could hardly disturb a baby in a crib."[27]

He continued:

> The record itself was somewhat revolutionary, in that it contained no songs, but two sides of sound effects collaged together with random voices. It was avant garde all right, and it sold primarily for its album cover."[28]

When an album contains no songs and is sold for its sexually exploitative cover, one has to wonder why. If our thesis is correct—that warfare is being waged to topple Western civilization through meaningless art and music—then it makes a great deal of sense.

Lennon's other rock albums and songs, however, made it very clear that "revolution is in the air."

Newsweek said, "Rock was the music of rebellion—against parents, against the establishment, against social restraints."[29]

Just as *Sgt. Pepper's* was the watershed of the drug culture in 1967, Lennon's *Sometime in New York City* was the watershed of the revolution in 1972. It set him squarely in the Marxist-Leninist camp, confirming a 1971 *Rolling Stone* interview in which he had said "Working Class Hero" was his contribuiton to the revolution and that Chairman Mao was his hero.[30]

Yet *Rolling Stone* commented:

> *Sometime in New York City* (1972), a disastrous double album of simplistic sloganeering (Lennon and Ono with the leftist bar band, Elephant's Memory) and senseless live jamming (Frank Zappa was among the players). Lennon's early wit and gift for aphorisms had tempo-

rarily turned into agitprop rhetoric that numbed the mind.[31]

The album was, indeed, agitation propaganda. Not only did the leftist band Elephant's Memory play a leading role, but Frank Zappa also had his hand in it.

Songs on the *Sometime* album included: "Sisters O Sisters" which speaks of the necessity to build a new world, but "we must learn to fight." In "Angela," Angela Davis was portrayed as a political prisoner. Her views and Lennon's views were said to be identical—and Angela Davis ran as a 1980 vice-presidential candidate on the Communist Party ticket!

"Woman is the Nigger of the World" portrayed woman as the slave of slaves. The accompanying illustration showed a demonic male knifing a woman. In "We're All Water," Richard Nixon and Mao danced in the nude. "Attica State" proclaimed "now's the time for revolution," and "Bloody Sunday" rings out—"you Anglo pigs and Scotties sent to colonize the North."

Lennon's "Give Peace a Chance" won favor from the Soviets and the entire International Socialist network since he apparently meant, "Give Communist Peace a Chance." The song was put together with Tommy Smothers, drug high priest Timothy Leary, a group of Hare Krishna singers, and Lennon and Yoko.

John Lofton noted,

The kind of "peace" Lennon and the movement wanted to give a chance to was given a chance . . . the result was the peace of the grave for millions. Following the withdrawal of U.S. military forces from Southeast Asia and the termination of U.S. support of our allies in that area, communists killed more than two million Cambodians and caused the drowning deaths of more than

150,000 South Vietnamese "boat people" in the South China sea.[32]

There is little doubt why Lennon and the Beatles were the left's "favorite cultural heroes."[33] Yet at the same time Lennon promoted the Marxist Leninist propaganda, he was accumulating a fortune of *over $250 million*. Lennon didn't practice what he preached.

Lennon was asked how he reconciled his vast wealth with his political philosophies. "You're supposed to be socialists, aren't you?" His reply, "I am . . . an instinctive socialist."[34] But still he insisted that he wanted to be rich.

In a *Newsweek* magazine interview Lennon was asked, "How do you look back on your political radicalism in the early '70s?" Lennon's reply:

> That radicalism was phony, really, because it was out of guilt. I'd always felt guilty that I made money, so I had to give it away or lose it. I don't mean I was a hypocrite—when I believe, I believe right down to the boots. . . . [But what] was I doing fighting the American government just because Jerry Rubin couldn't get what he always wanted—a nice cushy job.[35]

Lennon characterized his radicalism as phony since it was done out of guilt, but its effect was deadly real. Lennon, as spokesman for "the cause," believed in this cause "right down to his boots." But he felt betrayed by the Rubins who shouted for revolution yet joined the Wall Street establishment. He even felt betrayed by his own guilt over money.

But American troops were the ones truly betrayed by the Lennons, Rubins, and Jane Fondas—57,000 died trying to stop the Communist conquest of South Vietnam. Their deaths were real. The revolution was real, and Lennon was deeply involved.

He wanted it known that the Beatles were as revolutionary as the Rolling Stones. Regarding Lennon's involvement with the SDS, Fred Sparkes reported:

> Over drinks Lennon gave Hoffman and Rubin an envelope containing fifty $100 bills—$5,000—for 'the cause.' According to my sources, Lennon, the most radical Beatle, said he hoped some of the money would assist members of the SDS who are being sought for several bomb outrages.[36]

Singing "Working Class Hero," "Give Peace a Chance," "Back in the USSR," "Power to the People," and "Angela" on one hand, and singing drug lyrics and sexually immoral ditties on the other (plus giving money to the SDS, the IRA, and declaring Mao his hero) all add up to one conclusion—Lennon was a soldier of the revolution.

Lennon was asked, "What about the sexual puns: 'When you feel my finger on your . . .?'" Lennon replied, "Well it was at the beginning of my relationship with Yoko, and I was very sexually oriented then. When we weren't in the studios, we were in bed."[37]

In another interview he was asked, "You say the social revolution is going to happen out of the sexual revolution . . . in other words, everything in the social structure as it exists, you oppose?" Lennon answered, "Yes, agreed."[38] Lennon's sexual philosophy assumes crucial significance as it relates to his socially radical views.

Consider the sexual and political philosophy of Bianca Perez Moreno de Macias (Bianca Jagger). "I was brought up in a terrible way," she said. "Brainwashed by the sexual repression in Catholic Nicaragua, I was taught that virginity was the biggest asset in life, and I believed it."[39] But not for long! At age eighteen Bianca went to Paris to study political science at the Sorbonne and discovered liberation and the far left. Said Tony Sanchez:

> In Paris she rapidly surrendered her virginity and found the experience so pleasant that she began to question all the other conservative beliefs her parents had instilled in her. Like Jagger, she moved politically to the far left and began to dabble vicariously with revolution. For a while she was involved in the publication of a violently radical student magazine.[40]

The sexual revolution is the prelude to the social revolution. Sex is a powerful weapon, a weapon advocated by Herbert Marcuse, spokesman for the New Left: "The Marxian idea of socialism is not radical enough; *we must develop the moral, sexual rebellion of our youth* [italics added]."[41]

Permissiveness is a means for the demoralization necessary to effect social revolution (force being the sufficent condition).

One text on cultural subversion reads,

> Creating a greed for drugs, sexual misbehavior and uncontrolled freedom and presenting this to them as a benefit of communism will with ease bring about our alignment.[42]

Rock music unabashedly gives permission for drugs, sexual misbehavior, and total freedom to do whatever one wants to do! A radical at Essex University confirmed this vital link. "The new sexual permissiveness . . . sparked the student protest movement . . . in our Red Revolution."[43]

Dr. Timothy Leary envisioned this effect some years back. After having proclaimed himself a revolutionary, he called for the destruction of the present social struc-

ture and the establishment of a new hedonistic order—
"An esthetic, 'hedonic era' in which the symbol of the
messiah will be a nude couple and the purpose of life
will be pleasure."[44]

What Leary dreamed about, Lennon practiced. The
"messianic" nude couple bears strong resemblance to
The Two Virgins jacket photos. There is little speculation about Yoko Ono's sex life with John Lennon. Said
Newsweek, "Patrons at the Ritz, a New York rock
mecca, watch a videotape of the pair making love while
they listen to Yoko's new single, 'Walking on Thin
Ice.' "[45]

The sexual revolution is the struggle for total sexual
freedom without moral restraints. It is an attempt to
separate sex from love since love limits the expression
of sex. Although the sexual revolution has been around
for awhile, it is important to comprehend its medium as
well as its message. Its medium is pornography—"educational," hardcore, and musical. (Sex education without moral values is educational pornography; *Playboy*
and *Penthouse* are hardcore pornography; rock 'n' roll
is musical pornography.)

The message is more complicated. Dr. Ernest van den
Haag set the issue in perspective when he noted, "The
distinct social ideal of Western civilization since Christianity, has attempted to forge love, sex and commitment 'until death do us part.' "[46]

The sexual revolution declared war on this "archaic"
ideal, not only because the ideal is essentially Christian,
but because it is the contradiction of Lennon's philosophy: "What I want to do, I do; who I want to [expletive
deleted], I [expletive deleted].[47] "Man, I'd like to see a
little nakedness. Grab your friend and love him. There

are no laws. There are no rules."[48] Sex is no longer an expression of love. "The sexual revolution," said van den Haag, "is a change of attitude . . . the new attitude legitimizes and idealizes not love, but sex."[49]

He said, "Self-help manuals proclaim the independence of sex from love and marriage. Autonomous sex is thought to be liberated."[50] Pure sex, or "winged eros," is sex unrestricted by knowledge, conflict, personality, relationship, obligation, or commitment. Unrestricted sex—the ideal of the social revolution, the ideal of rock 'n' roll, the ideal of Karl Marx, Friedrich Engels, V. I. Lenin.

"Throughout *The Origin of the Family* [by Marx and Engels] it is obvious that sex and love are strangers in the city of Marxism,"[51] said H. Kent Geiger in *The Family in Soviet Russia*. Communism and greater sexual freedom are hand in glove since sexuality was closely connected to materialism while love was considered too metaphysical, or even a mere "physiological phenomenon of nature."[52]

Charles Hartshorne mentions this very thing when he said,

> Love has in it, as theology shows, a principle of infinity such that one cannot do justice to love among human beings, especially the most intimate and many-sided instances of this love, except by seeing in it a partial realization of what, in its fullness, would be divine.[53]

Analyzing *The Origin of the Family,* Geiger notes that sex is highly idealized and that the sexual life of the savage is favored over the so-called hypocritical restraints of civilized society. Adultery is praised.

"Socialism," said Lunacharski, onetime Soviet commissar of education, "brings with it new forms of relationships between men and women—namely free love."[54] Lunacharski explained:

> A man and a woman come together, live together while they like each other—and after they no longer like each other they depart. They are together for a relatively short period, not setting up a permanent household. Both the man and woman are free in this relationship.[55]

Geiger said the average Russian citizen looks upon the Communist and his way of life "not as a model of virtue and principle, but as purely and simply licentious."[56]

The "League of Free Love," organized by the Russian government, sought to convince the world that sexual freedom is (1) the Revolution's gift to the people, (2) the inevitable conclusion to Marx's naturalistic philosophy, (3) liberation from Christian restrictions on sex, and (4) synonymous with public ownership of property since monogamy is synonymous with private ownership of property.

"Husband, wife, children—husband and wife who bear and rear children, this is a bourgeois business,"[57] said Lunacharski. The old ethical norms went out with the old order. The new order and the new norms promised new happiness.

The problem, however, as the Marxists soon discovered, is that a society cannot survive without defined ethics. Although the Communists separated marriage from economics, destroyed the family hearth, and exposed the "hypocrisy" of the family, women soon discovered that sexual freedom benefited only the men who, happily whistling a tune of sexual liberation, abandoned their wives and children.

To prevent further disintegration of the family, the

Communists initiated the new family policy of the 1930s which made child rearing a legitimate family function, homosexuality a criminal offense (1934), and sexual promiscuity—easy marriages, bigamy, adultery—undesirably difficult (1935–36). Free love was declared bourgeois morality. Marx, Engels, and Lenin were no longer the authorities on family, love, and sex. Socialism—not sexual freedom—was made synonymous with a strong, healthy family. In fact, advocates of free love were considered enemies of the revolution:

> The enemies of the people, the vile fascist hirelings—Trotsky, Bukharin, Krylenko and their followers—covered the family in the USSR with filth, spreading the counter-revolutionary "theory" of the fall of the family, of disorderly sexual cohabitation in the USSR, in order to discredit the Soviet land.[58]

Nevertheless, the British musician who led hippie bands in the streets of St. Germain des Pres in Paris perceptively explained that "Rock 'n' roll, drugs, and Communism are all of the same essence."[59] Of course, he was thinking of the Marxist-Leninist stance on sexual liberation before the clock was turned back to the old Christian morality of "Thou shalt not commit adultery."

However, because the Bolsheviks decided that free love wasn't for them (at least for the moment) does not mean that free love isn't a most powerful piece of artillery to undermine non-Communist nations. While the Communists, for example, outlawed rock 'n' roll in the USSR, the Communist press insisted that young people in the USA deserved it.[60]

Susan Sontag explained that what may be acceptable before the revolution may not be acceptable after.

The American left is correct to be anarchic, because it is out of power. The freaky clothes, rock, drugs, sex, are pre-revolutionary forms of cultural subversion and so you can have your orgy, and still be moral and revolutionary. But in Cuba, the revolution has come to power, and so it follows that such disintegrative 'freedom' is inappropriate.[61]

Rock 'n' roll has played a large role in developing this evil sexual rebellion of our youth. Before moving over to Wall Street, Jerry Rubin insisted that, "Rock 'n' roll marked the beginning of the revolution."[62] He said, "We've combined youth, music, sex, drugs, and rebellion with treason, and that's a combination hard to beat."[63]

"Our role," said Ed Sanders of the rock group The Fugs, "is to influence teenagers with socially radical views."[64]

Our music, said Paul Kantner of the Jefferson Airplane, is intended to "change one set of values to another." This translates into "Free minds . . . free dope . . . free bodies [sex] . . . free music."[65]

Rock singer David Crosby said:

I figured the only thing to do was to swipe their kids. . . . By saying that, I'm not talking about kidnapping, I'm just talking about changing their value systems, which removes them from their parent's world very effectively.[66]

"The great strength of rock 'n' roll," said Marxist writer Irwin Silber, "lies in its beat . . . it is a music which is basically sexual, un-Puritan . . . and a threat to established patterns and values."[67]

"Rock radicalized teenagers," said rock producer

Martin Perlich, "because it estranges them from the traditional virtues which they no longer see as relevant."[68]

Lennon and his legacy have greatly aided this revolution. To repair the rent in the social fabric caused by Lennon and his legacy would require, at the minimum, an admission that pornography is not literature, that rock is not music, that sex is not love, that drugs are not the answer.

Seven

The Legacy

Rock 'n' roll is a multibillion-dollar assault on the moral foundation of civilized society.

Love, trust, compassion, caring, kindness, faithfulness, patience, self-control, purity, and goodwill are considered unnatural inhibitions from "the old order." Faithfulness for an hour or two is deemed more reasonable than lifelong commitment. The "free" life is regarded superior to the life in submission to God, marriage partner, and family.

Lennon's legacy of atheism, anarchy, hedonism, drugs, and revolution continues to gather momentum. Significant offspring of Lennon's legacy are "accepted" sexual abnormalities, bestiality, sadism, masochism, necrophilism, but especially homosexuality.

"I am . . . trying to produce songs to make gay people . . . acceptable"[1] boasts the producer/manager/composer of the homosexual rock group, Village People. Village People has been propagating the homosexual message for some time. Their very first album released in 1977 "featured four gay-oriented hymns to San Francisco, Hollywood, Fire Island and Greenwich Village."[2]

Since then the group has sold millions of records

promoting homosexuality, including "I'm a Cruiser," "YMCA," "In the Navy," and "Macho Man." The U.S. Navy at one time considered making a recruitment film of the Village People singing "In the Navy" until someone embarrassingly discovered that "cruising" was not synonymous with activity on a cruiser. ("Cruising" is a slang term used by gays to describe looking for a casual, one-night pickup.)

The Village People also helped launch disco rock, a music said to be "a . . . call for gays to come out of the closet."[3] Said *Newsweek,* "These trend-setting city discos are usually owned and operated by homosexuals."[4]

Although some may accept the notion that disco rock is merely a "symbolic" call for gays to dance together, others, like Dr. Frank M. duMas, see something more significant in the activity:

> Homosexuals sometimes use the rocking beat of modern music and the social pressures of large groups dancing in total abandon in order to break through the inhibitions of young, impressionable teenagers. Such modern "orgies" when carried on in public seem to have something in common with the St. Vitus Dance and Tarantism of the Middle Ages.[5]

Disco rock is sometimes referred to as "sex rock" although rock music also is certainly "sex rock." In disco, however, the words are less important than the pounding beat. Its sensuous, throbbing rhythms have been described by Robert Hilburn "as a temporary thrill . . . a night in a bordello."[6]

Newsweek described the music as follows: "From Latin music, it takes the percolating percussion, its sensuous, throbbing rhythms; from Afro and Cuban music, it repeats simple lyric lines like voodoo chants."[7]

With disco's "sex rock" came disco's sex dance sometimes called the "freak" dance or "the dance of death," "the dance of jealousy" or the troubleddance."

Reported *Parade* magazine, "When Jim Moore performed the Freak in Detroit with his girl friend, an incensed young man named Jimmie Rogers allegedly shot him in the chest three times."[8]

According to *Parade,* the Freak is danced by partners who bend their knees, spread their legs, advance upon each other with whirling hips until they touch. At this point, some couples retreat while others improvise.

John Parrikhal of Joint Communications Corporation of Toronto described disco rock as "music that fiddles while Rome burns."[9]

When Herbie Mann heard that disco music is "like a porno film," he sneered. Two disco hits later, however, he concluded, "I've come to like pornography."[10]

Pornography set to music is an apt definition of disco rock, and when one adds the ever present drugs you can nearly smell Rome burning. One top New York deejay combines laughing gas, pills, amyl nitrite, and marijuana and says "drugs really make the experience almost spiritual."[11]

Donna Summer, who now claims to be a born-again Christian, was disco's "First Lady of Lust." "Love to Love You Baby" feigns twenty-two orgasms. Lennon's hedonistic legacy was for real. He would have been proud of her. In fact, Yoko Ono simulated orgasm on the 1980 Lennon/Ono *Double Fantasy* album. Referring to "Kiss Kiss Kiss," Yoko said it is just the sound of a woman "coming to a climax."[12]

The change of the '80s envisioned by Lennon and Yoko is the era of the *Two Virgins* warmed over. But then John's philosophy had always been if we can't go nude or smoke pot, we're never going to get anywhere. Lennon was a consistent hedonist—a prophet of permissiveness. His legacy would not disappoint him.

Drugs, promiscuity, perversion, and revolution—the essence and message of rock 'n' roll.

Punk rock—so labeled because it is rough, rude, and raw—reflects the plunge into anarchy and nihilism. At its most abstract level, punk is a chip on the shoulder, "a clenched fist aimed at conformity and authority. At its most specific, punk can expound strick Marxist dogma—as long as it does so loudly and with a strong beat."13

At its less abstract level, punk is capsuled in Dukowski, Ginn, and Rollins' "No Values." It advocates destroying everything since there are no values, and therefore, "might as well blow you away."14

The Who is one of the most famous predecessors of punk rock. Peter Townshend refers to himself as "the aging daddy of punk rock."15 "In performance," said *Time,* "the band seems to play possessed."16 The Who became famous for smashing their instruments at the end of each performance. Drummer Keith Moon, who died of a drug overdose at the age of thirty-one, would blow up his drum set. Townshend would ram his guitar into his amp, and Roger Daltrey would slam his mike against the stage.

"Rock has always been demanding," said Townshend, "it is demanding of its perfomers and its audiences. And of society. Demanding of change."17

Townshend also claims that rock will kill him. "Mentally or physically or something, its going to get me in the end. It gets everybody in the end."18

It got a few Cincinnati fans in December, 1979. Eleven people were killed trying to get in to hear The Who. *Time* described Who audiences as some of the wildest in rock. A veteran Cincinnati music critic said it was the worst crowd he had ever encountered and vowed even before he learned of the deaths that he would never attend another such concert. He said that few are talking about the drinking and drugs as contributing factors in the slaughter.[19]

"Anarchy, that's what The Who is all about,"[20] said Robert Butler, music critic for the *Kansas City Times*. That's what punk rock is all about. Although the "Godfather of Punk," Lou Reed, has mellowed somewhat recently (left his boyfriend Rachel, married Sylvia, and is down to marijuana[21]), his punk rock contributions are still evident. RCA's "Lou Reed Rock 'n' Roll Animal," available at record counters, features such material as "Sweet Jane," "Heroin," and "White Light/White Heat." On the record jacket we're told: "When the smack begins to flow. . . ."

"Heroin [is] my life," sang Reed. As we saw earlier in the album *Street Hassle* recorded with Bruce Springsteen, Reed advised dealing with an overdosed girlfriend by placing her out in the street so that by morning she is just another hit and run.

Reed made it into the select Top Ten with his paean to sexual perversion and drug abuse called "Walk on the Wild Side." He courted fame in 1979 by mock-mainlining on stage.

Johnny Rotten's "Anarchy in the U.K." went to the top of the charts even though EMI (a record company) dropped the group and A&M not only dropped the group, but actually paid to get rid of them. The song says that he is an anti-Christ, and an anarchist who desires to kill and "bring anarchy in the U.K."

Punk rock nearly brought anarchy to the USA, too! John W. Hinckley, Jr., who attempted to assassinate President Ronald Reagan, was hooked on punk rock. Said the *Wall Street Journal,*

> While not much is known about his personal likes, he did have a reputation in Denver for liking rock 'n' roll music, and had recently been a fan of and attended a concert by his current favorite, a punk rock group called the Kamikaze Klones, who played such songs as "Death Can Be Fun," and "Psycho Killer."[22]

Edward Michael Richardson, also charged with threatening the President's life, is a marijuana smoker. He was smoking marijuana when he remarked to associates that it would be great if President Carter were shot. Richardson now claims that President Reagan will be shot to death and the country will be turned to the left.

Thousands of doped-up kids—similar to Europe's "Dead-End Kids" (Europe's counterpart to America's "Punk Rockers")—are accenting "self, not society" since "all society is rotten." Society is called rotten because it does not condone their counter-culture life-styles—especially with regard to drugs and sex. Drugs abound in Western Europe, and heroin is common on the streets where the philosophy is "Be free, be high, terror is a gas."

Punk rock is marketed by such established companies as CBS, Inc. (Columbia Records). In a recent ad announcing "The Psychedelic Furs," the blurb actually read, "A new album of beautiful chaos on Columbia records and tapes."[23] The ad ran in *Slash*, a punk rock publication.

In an interview that *Slash* conducted with the punk

group Crass (a British band, whose symbol is the X'd-out cross), one admitted that the police were investigating them for "criminal blasphemy," that is, for slandering the name of Christ. Since one of the band members has worn a tee shirt reading "Destroy Christianity," the charge isn't difficult to believe. Although Crass says it has no goals, it is obvious that it has at least one: to free their followers from the Christian ethic. Their complaint is that "everything is based around the Christian ethic,"[24] but the ethic is far beyond the apparent size of the Christian religion.

The latest punk-oriented film, *The Decline of Western Civilization* (1981), featured such punk rock groups as Alice Bag Band, Black Flag, Catholic Discipline, Circle Jerks, Fear, Germs, and X. The film fulfills the expectations of its title. It is, as *Los Angeles Times* critic Robert Hilburn said, "a nihilistic cesspool of intolerance and rage."[25] Black Flag dedicated a song to the Los Angeles Police Department which said "Revenge!/I'll watch you bleed. /Revenge! /That's all I read." Observed Hilburn,

Debauchery isn't new in rock, but it has usually been cloaked in a teasing veil of sex and drugs that, in the hands of a group like the . . . Stones, make it seem attractively evil. In "The Decline" there is little to covet . . . the music is often akin to the convulsion of a sick society.[26]

Penelope Spheeris, director of the film, views punk rock as the beginning of a new era. She noted that rock music "has always been a catalyst." It was in rock music that you could first detect change. She stated: "As time passed, you could see the movement kind of integrate itself into society."[27]

Darby Crash of the Germs played the lead role in the film. He lay incoherent on the stage, stoned. Before he arrived at that point, however, he sang, "If I am only an animal, Then I can do no wrong. But they say I'm something better, So I've gotta hold on." The song, Crash's "Manimal," complains that "evolution is a process too slow to save my soul."

According to Spheeris, Darby Crash "was real smart." Nevertheless, at twenty-two years of age, in December, 1980, Crash died of a drug overdose. Rebellion cost him his life.

The punk rock syndrome may well be the logical consequence of the Nietzche/Darwin ethic. Crash seemed to think so, and theologian Carl F. H. Henry probably would agree. "Western civilization," said Henry, "falls into fast-decaying generations when generations that know better lose their hold on the Bible."[28] Punk rock's thrust is to loosen Western civilization's hold on the Bible. As Malcolm Muggeridge said,

> Western civilization is in an advanced state of decomposition . . . with the media, especially television, governing all our lives . . . it is easily imaginable that this might happen without our noticing . . . by accustoming us to the gradual deterioration of our values.[29]

When sixteen-year-old Brenda Spencer opened fire on a crowded San Diego schoolyard and killed two and wounded nine, she simply said, "I just did it for the fun of it, I don't like Mondays." As Leopold Tyrmand pointed out in an article entitled "Toying with the Cultural Messages," about the same time as the Spencer incident, one of the best-selling records in America was a new album by the Ramones, a punk rock group, singing "I don't care 'bout poverty/All I care 'bout is me." "Related?" asked Tyrmand, "of course they are." He said that such music and films as *Midnight Express* (which glorifies heinous violence, pederasty, and drug smuggling) create

> a cultural climate that rapidly dissolves those obligations by which civilization lives and without which it cannot survive . . . Brenda lives her daily life with KISS, another rock group, a teenage ideological icon which proselytizes, "Lust, Sweat, and Sex."[30]

One tragic example of behavior to which punk rock contributes at least in part involved the death of a fourteen-year-old girl, Marcy Renee Conrad of Milpitas, California. She had been strangled to death and left lying off the road in the hills outside town. At least thirteen students went out to look at her body. One girl picked up the murdered girl's jeans, cut off a patch promoting a local rock station, and threw the jeans down along the side of the road. One student tried to cover the body with leaves. Another took his eight-year-old brother along to see the body. One boy went twice. Those who saw the body went back to class or to the pinball arcade. One went home to bed. Another student said he only cared about collecting the marijuana cigarette he had won on a bet that the body was real.

The *Sacramento Bee* wanted to know what made the students so callous, so small, so indifferent. What was in the lives of these teenagers that made them willing to participate in such macabre voyeurism and so unable to care. The *Bee* answered its own questions when it said,

> The shock is the shock of the encounter with icy indifference, the indifference of the kids in the first instance, but, much more importantly, of the culture that produced them. How did we lose them in this void of television and electronic games and punk rock and vio-

lence in which they seem to live? The depersonalization did not begin yesterday; it is not unique to this moment, yet it seems more complete—and they seem more alienated and isolated—than what we have ever known before.[31]

One of punk's most outrageous lead ladies is Wendy O. Williams of the Plasmatics. She is "newsworthy" because she performs clad only in shorts with electrical tape and shaving cream on her bosom. She was arrested by Milwaukee's vice squad for fondling "a sledge hammer suggestively after using it to smash a TV set."[32] She was acquitted by a Cleveland jury on an obscenity charge.

The insanity of it all would be more evident in saner times, but these are not sane times. When John Lennon stamped his approval on punk rock, continuing success was assured. Said John, "I love all this punky stuff. It's pure. I'm not, however, crazy about the people who destroy themselves."[33]

Lennon's reference to those destroying themselves was a reference to Sid Vicious of the Sex Pistols who killed his live-in American girlfriend with a hunting knife and then died of a drug overdose. After Vicious (John Simon Ritchie was his real name) murdered his girlfriend, the police officer who arrested him said he was "still as high as a space probe." His apartment was referred to as a "pigsty."

The world of punk is out of sync with civilization, order and harmony. Consider some of the names: Sex Pistols, Dictators, Stranglers, Laughing Dogs, Kamikaze Klones, Monster, Castration Squad, The Blasters, The Damned, Talking Heads, New York Dolls, Dead Boys, Flamin' Groovies, Clash, Crass, Black

Flag, Flesh Eaters, Thundertrain, Weirdo, Cortinas, Plasmatics, Fear, Homicide, and Voidoids.

"The threat of punk violence has been around for a long time," said Newport Beach officer Rich Long after investigating a stabbing that followed a punk rock concert. "But we didn't get too concerned until this stabbing incident. These punks are something else. They showed no remorse at all about the stabbing. They didn't give a hoot that the guy almost died."[34]

The philosophy behind punk rock is anarchistic and nihilistic. Pink Floyd's "The Wall" portrays each teenager as a brick in the wall. Suicide is championed in "Goodbye Cruel World." Young people kept it number one on the charts for seventeen weeks in 1980.

If kids listen to rock music advocating sadism, masochism, bestiality, Satanism, violence, suicide, rebellion, meaninglessness, drugs, and promiscuity, what type of personality can we expect?

Even if they should go to a modern art museum, it's punk on the walls instead of on the stage. In regard to punk rock music, Dada, and surrealistic art, Glen O'Brien's article "Notes on the Neon Nihilists" observed:

> In London during the height of punk rock (1977-78), I saw a massive exhibition of Dada and surrealism at the Hayward Gallery. The similarity between what was happening just across town was amazing. Dada and punk graphics were often practically indistinguishable. In context punk seemed like Dada taken to the streets. Which, in ways, it was.[35]

The human propensity to deny is nearly unfathomable. Whether in music or art, a world view emerges. Whoever said we are living in a post-Christian, atheistic age could well have been describing modern art, films, literature, and music. The point we must all consider is this: When will civilization reflect modern culture? When it does, as Malcolm Muggeridge noted, it will be the end of Christendom and the reality of John Lennon's dream. The rock 'n' roll industry is not a mere wart on the body politic. It is a cancer. It is hemlock.

Such necrophilic poison as "Cold Ethyl" by Alice Cooper involved making love to a dead woman. "She's cool in bed, She oughta be 'cos Ethyl's dead."[36] The paramour kept his love in a refrigerator.

Cooper followed this one with "I Love the Dead." "I love the dead, before they're cold. . . Their bluing flesh for me to hold, I never even knew your now rotting face, while friends and lovers mourn your civic grace, I have other uses for you darling. I love the dead."[37] The record was produced by Warner Brothers.

Cooper, whose real name is Vince Furnier, changed his name to match that of a seventeenth century witch, Alice Cooper.[38] His father is a preacher. Cooper became famous for his mock public executions, dousing audiences with beer and dollar bills, and mutilating chickens and baby dolls by pulling their arms, legs, and heads off and throwing the pieces to the crowd. He called his song "Dead Babies." His reason for such behavior? "All the audience wants is sex and violence," he said. "I know because I used to watch television all day."[39] His sadism is so well received, however, that he cannot fill all his engagements.

Commenting on Cooper's behavior, nationally syndicated columnist Bob Greene wrote, "We cannot be shocked . . . anymore . . . nothing is wrong or immoral if no one gets hurt." Greene observed, "The ABC . . . network put Alice Cooper's sex and violence show on one . . . night, and the next day no one was even talking about it."[40]

ABC also put Chuck Berry on, said Greene, and soon a whole audience was singing "I Want to Play with My [deleted]." Few thought anything about it.

Lennon's imagined utopia? Greene recognized what was lacking:

> But things did not get better. Heroin addiction and gonorrhea became so common that both were soon acceptable dinnertable conversation . . . all the sexual barriers came down, and we saw the manifestations everywhere. . . . But the psychiatrists reported that they were finding more people with serious sexual problems in this open society, not fewer.[41]

The sadistic theme neither began nor ended with Alice Cooper. KISS presented it to thirteen-year-olds on the front cover of "Love Gun." Only depraved rock stars, rock recording companies, and rock radio stations would do such a thing. And only uninformed or misinformed parents would allow their young to hear it!

The Beatles tried their hand in this bin of sadism too, but they were too early. (Had they waited until now, there would have been no trouble; they probably would have sold millions.) Their sadistic effort was the album *Yesterday and Today*. The original cover showed the Beatles in butcher's smocks holding chunks of bloody raw meat. Decapitated baby dolls and other parts of the body were scattered among them. The cover was so offensive that disc jockeys refused to play any songs on the album. Capitol Records was forced to recall it and put a new cover on the record.

Today that record cover would be readily accepted, even praised.

The original raw meat and dolls picture of the Beatles

is presently being offered in a special commemorative album. The album, *The Beatles Rarities,* states on its cover, "Contains rare photos including 'Butcher' shot." It is copyrighted by Capitol Records, 1980! "The photo for the album cover was sent from England (where the album wasn't released). The picture had the group dressed in butcher smocks and holding chunks of bloody meat and decapitated baby dolls. . . Now for the first time, the entire butcher photo is reproduced."

Symptoms of a sick society? It is Lennon's legacy with a vengeance!

In a recent Gallup Youth Survey teenagers were asked to choose the three top rock groups. First on the list was Queen. "Queen," in homosexual parlance, means an effeminate gay male. Queen produced the anthem of gay liberation, "We Are the Champions."

But Queen's "Get Down Make Love" has to rank at the bottom of the barrel. Elektra/Asylum Records, a division of Warner Communications, produced the album *News of the World,* porno set to music. Lead singer Fred Mercury said he felt like a devil on stage—perhaps because of their sacrilegious chorus, "All going down to see the Lord Jesus." Queen's *Body Language* album cover is already offending most decent people.

In Queen's song "Another One Bites the Dust," the words of the title are repeated several times at the end. Played backward, one hears "decide to smoke marijuana," over and over. Such backward masking techniques may well have subconscious implications. Dr. Hal C. Becker, founder and director of the Behavioral Engineering Center in Metairie, Louisiana, believes the mind can decipher the garble. Said Becker, "I don't doubt it would work, and I don't doubt it's being done."[42]

It is being done not only by Queen, but also by Led

Zeppelin. Even Black Oak Arkansas and ELO are involved. Tom Gondolf, chief engineer for Goodnight Audio, Dallas, Texas, said, "Quite often on certain pieces of music they will put something in backward."[43]

The teens second choice on the Gallup poll was the rock group Led Zeppelin. Its lead guitar player, Jimmy Page, is the one who said that "Rock 'n' roll is [deleted] you music." To emphasize this point he charged the portals of decency with "Whole Lotta Love" and "Black Dog."

Page also has other interests, such as the occult. He purchased Aleister Crowley's mansion in Scotland and operates a bookstore rich in the occult. Said Page, "There was not one good collection of books on the occult in London and I was tired of having to go all different places to get the books I wanted."[44]

Crowley, a heroin addict and sexual pervert, was recognized as one of the most successful practitioners of black magic in this century. He referred to himself as "The Beast 666." Crowley not only impressed Page, but also the Beatles! His picture (and that of Karl Marx) is on the cover of the Beatles album *Sgt. Pepper's Lonely Hearts Club Band*.

Consider the following bizarre chain of events and personalities.

One of Crowley's disciples was Kenneth Anger, a personal friend of Mick Jagger of the Rolling Stones. It was Anger who introduced Jagger to the occult, and when Jagger discovered that "Satanism sells records,"[45] he went deeper and deeper into it. Jagger would appear as Satan and the Antichrist on stage, and his "Sympathy for the Devil" and "Dancing with Mr. D" (the devil) reflected his theology.

Kenneth Anger's dream, not surprisingly, was to produce a film glorifying the devil. It was to be called *Lucifer Rising*. He chose a young guitar player with the California rock band Love named Bobby Beausoleil to play Lucifer.

After filming for some time, Beausoleil went off the deep end and committed a bestial murder, including writing on the wall with his victim's blood. Beausoleil was a follower of Charles Manson, who was known to listen to the Beatles *White* album and especially "Helter Skelter." Manson later sent his troops over to murder actress Sharon Tate and her friends.

After Beausoleil was jailed for murder, Kenneth Anger turned to Mick Jagger to play the role of Lucifer. Jagger refused, but he did agree to write the music for it. It finally emerged under the title *Invocation to My Demon Brother*.

Led Zeppelin's Jimmy Page, however, has to rank as one of the most clever practitioners of the black arts. While Mick Jagger is obvious ("Sympathy for the Devil"), Page is subtle but deadly ("Stairway to Heaven").

Page's "Stairway to Heaven," though voted rock 'n' roll's most popular song of its twenty-five-year history, has nothing to do with the heaven of the Bible. It is the heaven of the occult.

The song begins with a woman climbing a stairway to heaven. When she arrives, she can get what she came for. The song insists that the pied piper will, through reason, lead us to a new day. "There are two paths you can go by" says the song, but there is still time "to change the road you're on." What road or path should we be on? The song concludes that if we listen hard, the true message will come to us at last.

I listened hard and the true message did not come.
The word did not come. The day to the new day dawn-
ing did not come. The new way, road, or path did not
come. That is, the hard-to-come-by message did not
come through while listening to the song played forward. But the message was clear when the record was
played backward (sometimes called back masking).

Where the song says "There are two paths you can go
by," stop the record and play it backward. You will hear
the message we must heed to find "heaven." It says,
"Here's to my sweet Satan." "There was a little child
born naked . . . now I am Satan." Elsewhere on the
backward side it says, "I will sing because I live with
Satan." If you listen hard the true message will come,
says the song. The tune is Satan. He is the word. His
way will bring forth a new day, a way of reason will
replace the West's way of God, the Bible, morality. The
piper, Jimmy Page, is calling us to join him and establish
the occult's heaven on earth!

Jimmy will be helped in this attempt by John Travolta
and Olivia Newton–John. They plan to team up again
for a screen version of the musically based "Stairway to
Heaven" by Columbia Pictures. Richard Rush will produce and direct.[46]

However, it might not be smooth sailing because California Assemblyman Phil Wyman is calling for a full
investigation into backward masking. Mr. Wyman has
introduced a bill (No. 3741) into the California legisla-
ture which would require record companies to place
warning labels on the record jackets stating the following: "Warning: This record contains backward masking
which may be perceptible at a subliminal level when the
record is played forwards." Congressman Robert Dor-

nan of California has introduced a similar bill into the U.S. Congress.

Assemblyman Wyman not only specifically mentions "Stairway to Heaven," but also Styx's "Snowblind," which says, "O Satan move in our voices," ELO's "El Dorado," which says, "Christ, you're the nasty one, you're inferno," and Black Oak Arkansas's, "Raunch 'n' Roll," which says, "Satan, Satan, Satan, he is god."

On the inside of the jacket or record sleeve of "Stairway to Heaven" is a picture of a mountain, a druid priest shining his occult light, a struggling young woman looking up to the light with a goat (the goat's head is the universal symbol of Satan worship), and a walled castle in the background.

In druid mythology, young virgin women were sacrificed to appease Satan. On the front cover of the album is a picture of an old man with a bundle of sticks. You can almost smell the pyre burning and the sacrifice completed as the innocent young woman thinks she is following the liberating light of the druid priest.

The song and album are odes to the occult and Satanism. McCandlish Phillips commented:

> Occultism and idolatry go together. There is a direct connection between idolatry and demonic supernaturalism, and Satan is the head of it all. It is all part of his vast conspiracy to overthrow the worship of God.[47]

Although Page knows that the black arts, magic, witchcraft, and the psychic are satanic in origin, naive young people do not. Many are unaware of the Bible's admonition to "not practice . . . witchcraft."[48] This prohibition would also include not buying albums promoting witchcraft.

Phillips also noted that some demonic religions sacrifice their young by burning them to death. Again the Bible condemns such activity,

> There shall not be found among you any one who burns his son or his daughter as an offering, any one who practices divination, a soothsayer, or an augur, or a sorcerer, or a charmer, or a medium, or a wizard, or a necromancer. For whoever does these things is an abomination to the Lord; and because of these abominable practices, the Lord your God is driving them [the nations] out before you."[49]

The occult has found a friendly welcome in the rock world, and two other famous groups, Black Sabbath and Blue Oyster Cult, have had great success selling Satan rock. Black Sabbath never hid their Satanic allegiance from the public. The cross of Christ was placed upside down on their first album. "Sabbath, Bloody Sabbath" clearly showed the number "666," the mark of the beast. After a concert in Tulsa, Oklahoma, the *Tulsa World* music critic wrote, "Black Sabbath sang about the occult, death and drugs."[50] Lead singer (at that time) Ozzy Osbourne, however, is now concerned whether he may be a medium for some outside force. Said Osbourne, "Whatever it is, frankly, I hope it's not what I think—Satan."[51] The Blue Oyster Cult's "Don't Fear the Reaper," a song about two teenage sweethearts planning to commit suicide, reveals their morbid affections.

Both Blue Oyster and Black Sabbath were involved in a riot in Milwaukee's Arena in October 1980. In one night, 160 persons were arrested, half on drug charges, and the arena suffered a $10,000 property loss. Young people overturned chairs, ripped out seat cushions, pulled out iron railings, lit firecrackers and small fires, vandalized telephones and fire extinguishers, knocked out lighting fixtures, and threw objects around the arena.

Bob Larson's *Rock* specifies the occult involvement of: The Eagles, Jimi Hendrix, Jefferson Starship, Rainbow, Led Zeppelin, Fleetwood Mac, Earth, Wind and Fire, Stevie Wonder, Daryl Hall, Van Morrison, Al Jardine, Steve Hackett, Jackson Browne, Tangerine Dream, Dr. John, Cat Stevens (now a convert to Islam), Meat Loaf, Nazareth, Santana, Queen, David Bowie, Heart, and Rolling Stones. Larson says yesterday's vices were sex and alcohol, "today's entertainment heroes have added another—the Devil."[52]

The occult implications, for example, of the following albums and records are obvious: The Rolling Stones' "Their Satanic Majesty's Request," "Goat's Head Soup," "Sympathy for the Devil" and 'Dancing with Mr. D"; Styx' "Snowblind" ("Oh Satan move in our voices" when played backward); The Eagles' "Hotel California"; Earth, Wind, and Fire's "All in All"; Fleetwood Mac's "Bare Trees," "Born Enchanters"; Rush's "Witch Hunt" and "Necromancer"; AC/DC's "Highway to Hell," "C.O.D. (Carry Out the Devil)," and "Evil Walks"; Ozzy Osbourne's "Blizzard of Ozz" and "Diary of a Madman"; Grateful Dead's "Friend of the Devil" and Iron Maiden's "Killers."

The third choice of American teens is AC/DC. AC/DC, in slang terminology, refers to bisexual activity. The group denies this association as unfounded rumor, ostensibly intending the electrical unit connection rather than the sexual. Even so, their songs ("You Shook Me All Night Long," "Dirty Deeds Done Dirt

Cheap," "Let Me Put My Love into You") are so offensive that decency prohibits printing excerpts from their lyrics.

Keep in mind that these are the top three rock groups as selected by American teens! With such groups propagating "the word," does it really take much wisdom to discern our direction? Gadara? How about Gehenna?

The Dr. Hook band is seen daily in the Los Angeles area on one of the cable outlets. A few years back it spoke to youth on ABC's Wide World of Entertainment—and what a message. Hook's album *Sloppy Seconds*—produced by CBS Records, copyrighted by Evil Eye Music, Inc. (an excellent hint of what's inside)—derived its name from a homosexual expression.

One song tells us "We've got a freaky old lady named Cocaine Katy" and also talks about the band's teenage groupies and pill-taking. Another song tells us they dream of "chicks," "animals," and "boys"—sexism, bestiality, and homosexuality in just four lines. But even this appears mild when compared to "Freaker's Ball," which describes a perverted party for fags, dikes, leather freaks, sadists, masochists, necrophiliacs, and pyromaniacs. Among other things, we're told, "I'll kiss yours if you'll kiss mine."

Both Plato and Aristotle understood the deadliness of this type of music four hundred years before Christ.

Plato wrote in *The Republic*,

When modes of music change, the fundamental laws of the state always change with them [for] this spirit of licence [lawlessness], finding a home, imperceptibly penetrates into manners and customs; whence, issuing with greater force, it invades contracts between man and man, and from contracts goes on to laws and constitutions, in utter recklessness, ending at last, by an overthrow of all rights, private as well as public.[53]

Plato concluded, "If amusements become lawless, and the youths themselves become lawless, they can never grow up into well-conducted and virtuous citizens."

Aristotle, in his last three chapters in *Politics*, also spoke to the likes of Dr. Hook, Cooper, AC/DC, Led Zeppelin, Queen, Village People, Rolling Stones, and the Beatles. His comments could be printed in today's newspaper as describing the effects of rock 'n' roll. He said,

> Emotions of any kind are produced by melody and rhythm . . . music has the power to form character . . the manner of its arrangement being so important that the various modes may be distinguished by their effects on character. One, for example, working in the direction of melancholy, another of effeminacy; one encouraging abandonment, another self-control, another enthusiasm; and so on through the series.[54]

Aristotle's references to the effeminate covers much of disco rock, Queen, Village People, Rolling Stones' "Sucking in the Seventies," and Prince's "Dirty Mind." Elton John said, "There's nothing wrong with going to bed with somebody of your own sex. I just think people should be very free with sex—they should draw the line at goats."[55] David Bowie was one of the first rock stars to admit his homosexuality publicly, although he also said, "Love is a disease that breeds jealousy, anxiety, and brute anger."[56]

Rolling Stone said that Prince's album *Dirty Mind*, produced by Warner Brothers, may be the most generous album about sex ever made by man. "Prince lets it all hang out . . . the major tunes are paeans to bisexuality, incest and [deleted] technique. . . . This is lewdness cleansed by art."[57] Yet, by the end of 1981 *Newsweek* had already crowned Prince the "Prince of Rock," a prophet of sexual anarchy. Prince apparently believes in salvation through sex. His new-age revelation is "the second coming—anything goes." *Newsweek* said "he just may be the most exciting new star in pop music today."[58]

"Sex is where it's at in music,"[59] said Johnny Bristol. "Rock and roll is ninety-nine percent sex,"[60] said John Oates. "When you're in a certain frame of mind particularly sexually oriented, there's nothing better than rock and roll, because that's where most of the performers are at,"[61] said David Kreb of Aerosmith.

"Everybody takes it for granted rock and roll is synonymous with sex,"[62] said Chris Stein of Blondie. "I've always thought that the main ingredients in rock are sex,"[63] said Debbie Harry of Blondie. "Pop music is sex and you have to hit them [teenagers] in the face with it,"[64] said the Rolling Stones' manager. "The language, the argot of rock is grounded in sexuality,"[65] said Sara Davidson. "The stage is our bed and the audience is our broad," said the Jefferson Airplane. "We're not entertaining, we're making love."[66] Convinced? If not, listen to Olivia Newton–John tell about her "body talk" in "Let's Get Physical," or try the J. Geils Band in "Centerfold." The Associated Press (March 5, 1982) mentioned these songs and others in an article entitled, "Rock bands putting out X-rated music."

We noted earlier that the late Jim Morrison of The Doors said, "Man, I'd like to see a little nakedness around here. Grab your friend and love him. There are no laws. There are no rules."[67] It was Morrison who wanted to be thought of as an "erotic politician." I am interested, he said, "in anything about revolt, disorder, chaos, especially activity that has no meaning."[68]

"The Rev. Jesse Jackson," said *Rolling Stone* magazine, "is calling very loudly for a ban on the Rolling Stones' 'Some Girls,' citing it as racist and sexist, especially the lines, 'Black girls just want to get [expletive deleted] all night.'"[69]

Jackson had more in mind than just "Some Girls," however. He also mentioned "Shake Your Booty," "Ain't Love a Bitch," "I Want to Do It to You All Night Long," "Let's Spend the Night Together," "I Want to Do Something Freaky to You," "It's All Right to Make Love on the First Night," "Squeeze Box" and "Love to Love You Baby." Said Jackson,

> Our responsibility as a movement must be met by speaking out against the people who are putting these songs on the air and into the stores. Our children's minds are adversely affected and there is a definite correlation between the rising rate of illegitimacy and increasing numbers of abortions and songs about sex.[70]

Fifteen years earlier Dr. Ronald Sprangler, Chief School Medical Officer, Nottingham, England, spoke similar words. "Teenage pop music," he said, "was probably to blame for the mounting obsession with sex." Sara Davidson pointed out, "There is some of the groupie in almost every girl who watches a rock singer in leather pants and metal hardware, snapping his body and making a sound so loud it is very near pain."[71]

Patricia Schiller, a psychologist and director of the American Association of Sex Education and Counselors, measured the erotic effects of the music media. She found that youngsters were listening to the lyrics and finding them provocative and arousing.

In her studies she noted a number of girls (ages 12–21) who admitted that the insistent beat and the suggestive lyrics excited them to take part in sex play and lovemaking. Although older girls were better able to handle their instinctive desires, twelve- and thirteen-year-olds could not. The younger girls were psychologically disturbed and seemed to have trouble expressing their feeling.

It began with the Beatles' "Let's Do It in the Road," "Gimme Gimme What You Got," "Penny Lane," "I'm Only Sleeping," and "Baby You Can Drive My Car"; the Rolling Stones' "Let's Spend the Night Together," "Let It Bleed," and "I Can't Get No Satisfaction"; or other songs like "Group Grope," "Light My Fire," "Fillmore East," "Let It All Hang Out," "Rhapsody in the Rain," "Venus in Furs."

Today it is Rod Stewart's "Hot Legs" and "Do Ya Think I'm Sexy," KISS' "Love Gun," Alice Cooper's "Muscle of Love," Pink Floyd's "The Wall," Elton John's "All the Girls Love Alice," Exile's "Kiss You All Over," Ted Nugent's "Scream Dream," AC/DC's "You Shook Me All Night Long," The Knack's "Good Girls Don't (But I Do)" and "Baby Talks Dirty," Meat Loaf's "Paradise by the Dashboard Light," Pretender's "Precious," Billy Joel's "Only the Good Die Young," and Billy Thorpe's "In My Room."

Tomorrow?

If you think this analysis too prudish, consider Ann Landers's opinion. "I've been hearing about the filthy rock and roll lyrics for a long time," she said, "and decided to tune in and listen. Twenty-three years of this column have made me virtually shock-proof, but some of the lyrics were incredibly crude and offensive."[72]

An ABC executive put it like this: "A lot of rock

music is simply too sexy for TV. The aggressively sexual style of many groups and individual rock stars is one reason for their infrequent appearances on TV."[73]

In October 1977 *U.S. News And World Report* carried an article entitled "Flood of X-Rated Music Hits Airwaves, Concert Halls, Record Shops":

> Hot-selling songs with sexually explicit lyrics are moving up on the charts—causing widespread concern about effects on youth across the U.S.[74] At the heart of the furor is a wave of new songs that are sexually explicit . . . Unlike X-rated movies and books, this music is broadcast, performed in concert and available on records to any listener, regardless of age.[75]

Since this was written some record jackets have been printed with this announcement, "The album includes lyric content which may be offensive to some members of the public." Ted Nugent's *Scream Dream* album produced by CBS, Inc., included this warning label. However, the record is still available for purchase by juveniles.

"The rock music industry is leading millions of teenagers and young adults down the evil path of drugs, sexual promiscuity, and social irresponsibility,"[76] said Jack Carey, a former top-rated disc jockey in Baltimore, Buffalo, and Moline, Illinois. He quit because he could no longer tolerate playing blatantly sexual materials over the air.

When Carey resigned his boss said to him, "Look, Jack, you and I both know the record [Kiss You All Over] is a piece of [expletive deleted]. But there's a lot of that stuff in this industry."[77] But Carey was convinced that the rock industry was becoming too irresponsible with the messages it delivers to its young fans.

"Mick Jagger doesn't have to write music that's degrading and aimed at doped-up, mixed-up people. Why make hay at the expense of people who are wallowing in misery?"[78] said Carey.

His point is well taken—except we need to remember that it was rock music that set the cultural climate for drugs, degradation, and social irresponsibility in the first place. Parents who have seen their own flesh and blood waste away on drugs and finally commit suicide or overdose probably would not demur.

Lennon's legacy of rock and drugs has not subsided. According to *TV Guide*, "The average rock musician likes to perform [in an environment] of stomping, cheering crowds, typically well-dosed with alcohol and marijuana."[79]

Legalize It is a rock album produced by Columbia Records. The cover pictures Peter Tosh of the Wailers sitting in a field of marijuana and smoking grass. I purchased it April 8, 1981, along with Lou Reed's *Heroin* album, in a "respectable" rock 'n' roll center, which also featured drug-oriented messages and drug paraphernalia.

The following comments by a parent who attended a Ted Nugent rock concert in 1979 not only describe the Nugent concert, but most rock concerts.

Marijuana smokers were everywhere. If you were not smoking you were in the minority. Everyone milled and visited and passed around roaches and smoked a little more. . . . After intermission the audience was greeted by Ted Nugent saying "Are you high?" To which the audience replied, "Yea." His next statement was, "We're going to have a [expletive deleted] free for all." . . . It was plain to see almost everyone was high by that time.[80]

113

Tony Sanchez described a typical Rolling Stones concert. "Drugs were everywhere," he said, "jars of cocaine, uppers and downers."[81] Jagger, he said, was snorting quantities of cocaine before every show. Said Sanchez, "he felt he couldn't get up there to dance and scream without the high of the drug tearing through his body." Another Stones player was fixed on heroin. The songs of these tours are for sale today in the new Rolling Stones album, *Hot Rocks, 1964–71*.

"I can sing better after shooting smack in both arms,"[82] Linda Ronstadt once said. "Fleetwood Mac's John McVie was busted for cocaine and faces a $10,000 fine and/or ten years in jail,"[83] reported *Rolling Stone*. "The Grateful Dead's music is intimate, cosmic, spacey, laid back, obviously drug-influenced,"[84] said Vern Stefanic. "Black Sabbath sang about the occult, death and drugs."[85] "Drugs . . . make the experience almost spiritual,"[86] said a disco deejay. "I'm in the music business for the sex and the narcotics,"[87] said Glenn Fry of the Eagles. Glenn's partner Don Henly was fined $2,500 after pleading no contest to a charge of giving drugs to a sixteen-year-old girl found nude in his home.[88] "We avoid all hard drugs like cocaine," said the Bee Gees, "although we do smoke marijuana now and again."[89] "We were sitting, passing around a joint—a doobie—so we called ourselves the Doobie Brothers,"[90] said Tom Johnston. "Drugs are a necessary ingredient for many rock musicians,"[91] said Robert Forbes.

"Working in the rock world and refusing to use cocaine are rather like joining a rugby club and preaching total abstinence," said Tony Sanchez. He also said, "There are an awful lot of rock people who would find it hard to start the day without the adrenalin-provoking, rocket-fuel burst of a quick snort of about $30 worth of coke."[92]

The U.S. Department of Health, Education, and Welfare agrees, "The rock scene is permeated by the values and practices of the drug culture. Many rock stars have become cult heroes, and many of them take drugs . . . Rock concerts pose an additional problem . . . drugs are sold and used openly at these concerts." Few government agencies have addressed the relationship of drugs and the rock industry. And only one or two senators and congressmen have addressed the issue in spite of the fact that it is an issue, as Plato warned, that could well imperil the whole state. Lee Dogoloff, former White House drug policy adviser, remarked,

> If the present adolescent drug-abuse trends continue, we could soon acquire an unmanageable number of emotionally, intellectually and socially handicapped young people. We could have a 'diminished generation' unable to function effectively, if at all, in an increasingly complex and demanding world. In the area of adolescent drug abuse, therefore, we have neither the luxury of time nor the opportunity for esoteric debate.[93]

But Lennon's rock legacy and legions of fans could care less. For them Lennon's word is sufficient: "If people can't face up to the fact of other people being naked or smoking pot, or whatever they want to do, then we're never going to get anywhere."[94] This translates into "Drugs and sex and rock 'n' roll is all my brain and body needs" by Ian Dury or Richie Furay's comment . . . "decadent and drug-filled world of rock music."

Eight

The Challenge

Western civilization, its institutions, its moral values, are under increasing attack. We are tottering on the brink of spiritual suicide and a return to barbarism. Malcolm Muggeridge has already written a book entitled *The End of Christendom*.[1]

We must meet the challenge of cultural warfare against our system of morality, a system rooted in the Decalogue (the Ten Commandments) and the tenets of the Christian religion. Christianity's ethical ideals thwart hedonism's pleasurable appeals.

"People call me rude," sings Prince. "I wish we all were nude/I wish there was no black and white/I wish there were no rules."[2] Do we want to live under a biblical code which combines love, sex, and morality? Or do we wish to replace this with a "freer" moral code under which everyone is free to do his or her own thing?

This is the crux of the matter. A choice between two lifestyles based on widely differing world views.

We can choose a moral order reflecting the Ten Commandments, the Golden Rule, and biblical admonitions to love God with all our heart and our neighbor as ourself. We can choose a political order reflecting the U.S. Constitution and the Bill of Rights.

Or we can choose a moral order advocated by rock 'n' roll —drugs, permissiveness, pornography, perversion—and a political order based on anarchy or, as Lennon once advocated, a system of no government, police, or money.

To accept Lennon's "freer" society of nudity, sex on demand, pornography, and drugs is to accept anarchy, slavery, and death—not freedom.

Rock stars who lived—and died—according to the values espoused in Lennon's songs include Jimi Hendrix, Jim Morrison (The Doors), Elvis Presley, Janis Joplin, Brian Jones (Rolling Stones), Al Wilson (Canned Heat), Gram Parsons (Uriah Heep), Gary Thain (Uriah Heep), Vinnie Taylor (Sha Na Na), Keith Moon (The Who), Lowell George (Little Feat), Tommy Bolin (Deep Purple), Sid Vicious (Sex Pistols), Robbie McIntosh (Average White Band), Bon Scott (AC/DC), John Bonham (Led Zeppelin), James Honeyman Scott (The Pretenders), and Darby Crash (Germs).

They all lived according to Lennon's creed *and died young!*

When Lennon's word was put into practice at Altamont (Altamont is a tragic example of a "freer" society in miniature), the results were described by a Rolling Stones fan as: "a murderous reality of anarchy," and something "ugly, mindless, blind, black and terrifying."[3]

Modern films, literature, art, and music are pursuing the same "free" society. The message is identical and the results predictable. Lennon's own philosophy produced his murderer. President Reagan's accused assassin was also a product of this same lifestyle.

Lennon's word does not spell "Life." The world, the flesh, and the devil never do.

Lennon's "freer" society does not spell freedom. Millions hooked on drugs will find this out—thousands already have, but their deaths rarely trigger insight. Too often we look upon drug fatalities as simply accidental victims but nothing more.

Free sex, too, certainly isn't free—especially for the female who must decide whether to abort the "product of conception," give birth, marry the father, or bid him farewell.

Many of the so-called moral and political "freedoms" demanded by the avante garde were established in the USSR after the Bolshevik revolution in 1917, but (as noted in the chapter on "The Radical") these "freedoms" proved destructive to society and were removed. Not even the "League of Free Love" could make them work. C. S. Lewis' *Abolition of Man* says why. Karl Menninger's *Whatever Became of Sin* tells why. So does the Bible.

Although Lennon never mentioned sin (he undoubtedly agreed with the idea that man's evil propensity is merely a result of "a prehistoric vestige: a reptilian brain"[4]), it is, according to the Bible, the very heart of our troubles. Sin causes us to rebel against God and His ways. Sin causes us to seek pornography, promiscuous sex, drugs and perversion. Sin causes greed, envy, hate, murder and selfishness.

Rock 'n' roll glorifies fallen human nature. It appeals to our baser instincts—it doesn't lift up, it pulls downward. It doesn't inspirit, it denies spirit. It accents flesh, body, muscle, gland, organ. It's a body trip with passion in control. "There's no such thing as a secure, family-oriented rock 'n' roll song,"[5] insisted Mick Jagger.

Anthropologist J. D. Unwin remarked that human society is free to choose between sexual freedom and great energy but that no society could have both for more than one generation. The reason, undoubtedly, is sin. Once we dissipate ourselves on sex, drugs, and pornography, there is no social contribution left.

It should be obvious that our problem is moral, spiritual, and theological. Lennon's demand for a new social order proceeded from his theological base. Everyone's ultimately does.

So again the question: what kind of society do we want? One based on hedonism? Or one based on theism and morality? If the answer is hedonism, we need do nothing regarding modern films, literature, art, and music. However, if the answer is theism and morality, then we must appraise "the new day coming."

Before noting specific action to challenge rock's hedonism, we must face the greater challenge of creating a positive Christian culture. It is imperative for Christians to create art, literature, films, and music that glorify God and uplift the human spirit.

Unfortunately, what we are seeing today is the Christian message laminated to rock music. Christian rock and Christian punk rock (yes, there is such a thing) disguise two more nails in the coffin of Western civilization.[6] We don't need more rock music—pagan or Christian. We need a transfusion and infusion of solid Christianity.

How can we put out the rock-incited conflagration that is burning down our society.[7] Some people will resist a solution to the X-rated and drug drenched music because there are billions of dollars to be made exploiting kids. Moreover, those who presently enjoy such music and drugs don't want their lifestyle threatened. They do not care that society is threatened. ("It's Yoko and me/that's reality.")

THE CHALLENGE

Our first challenge is to discover exactly *what* is happening. Personal knowledge is essential. Listen to your local rock station for a few hours. (Some stations advertise in the local newspaper and tell you when to listen for AC/DC's "Dirty Deeds Done Dirt Cheap.") You probably will disbelieve your ears when you hear Billy Thorpe break loose with his famous "In My Room" song from his 1980 *21st Century Man* album produced by Elektra/Asylum Records, a division of Warner Communications. This album is a good example because it typifies both drug and X-rated emphases.

Thorpe begins by lighting up a joint (marijuana) because he wants to "get outta my head in my room." Following his drug "trip" he "makes love" to the centerfold model in his porno magazine. The song concludes with Billy calling Angela Browning to his room to play doctors and nurses, husband and wives— "wrapped in her ecstasy, as she gave me my manhood, I took her virginity."

Next, visit your largest rock record shop. Notice that the shop may also sell drug paraphernalia under the guise of novelty items. (This reinforces the close connection between drugs and rock 'n' roll.) Check the roach holders, marijuana papers, bongs and water pipes to cool the hot smoke, the stash cans. Check the thousands of albums. Check the Beatles selections and notice the brand new *Sgt. Pepper's* albums available. Drug albums are big business. Check John Lennon's "word" for our youth. Note the huge Rolling Stones selections. "Rape of the mind" is not an exaggeration. From Abba and AC/DC to the Wailers and Voidoids, the groups are extolling drugs, sexual anarchy, perversion, violence. And remember, *all this is readily available to your seven-year-old.*

Spend some time at your favorite newspaper and magazine shop. Browse through the magazines catering to the rock industry: *Rolling Stone, Circus, Creem, Hit Parader*. Reading just a few issues of *Rolling Stone* magazine will enable you to catch the flavor of the rock world. You might also consider reading Tony Sanchez's *Up and Down with the Rolling Stones* for an inside look at the morally bankrupt Stones, or Bob Larson's *Rock*[7] for another view of the rock culture.

Dr. John Diamond, a New York physician, has been studying the relationship between rock music and our physiological constitution. Diamond discovered that certain forms of rock music heighten stress and anger, reduce output, increase hyperactivity, weaken muscle strength, and could well play a role in juvenile delinquency. The beat used by rock groups such as the Rolling Stones, The Doors, Queen, Alice Cooper, Janis Joplin, and Led Zeppelin is a stopped anapestic rhythm (short-short-long). According to Diamond, this beat is *the exact opposite* of our heart and arterial rhythm. He is worried about the millions of people who are exposed hour after hour to rock music and are thus continually "switched" (a medical expression meaning that symmetry between the two hemispheres of the brain is lost, a serious matter since they are in a perpetual state of rhythmical swing day and night) and "stressed."[8]

While Dr. Diamond played rock music to humans, Dorothy Retallack played Led Zeppelin to plants. Her experiments were conducted under the supervision of her biology professor at Temple Buell College, Denver. She discovered that plants could take four weeks of Led Zeppelin, one of today's most popular rock groups, before they died! "In every experiment, none of which lasted more than four weeks, soothing melodies seemed to make the plants flourish. Loud and discordant sounds make them droop, then die."[9] Rock music seemed to cause erratic growth and erratic directional behavior in plants. Semi-classical or soothing music seemed to cause uniform, slightly larger growth than those plants not exposed to any music. After only ten days (three hours a day) of listening to Led Zeppelin, the plants were leaning away from the speaker (plants listening to calm devotional and soothing music were leaning toward the music!). At the end of three weeks the plants were dying, "the squash had almost fallen over. The morning glory, instead of crawling up as is natural, had sagged and was stretched over four pots in the direction away from the music. Corn stalks sagged in the middle."[10] Retallack questioned, "If rock music has an adverse effect on plants, is the rock music listened to so long and so often by the younger generation partly responsible for their erratic, chaotic behavior?"[11]

The local rock radio station is the linchpin holding the wheels of the rock industry firm. If the local station does not play rock, young people will not buy the records. If teens do not buy, the record company suffers. If the record company suffers, the rock star or band suffers.

All local rock stations have two potential soft spots: (1) the Federal Communications Commission which grants the station its license to operate, and (2) the sponsors who advertise on the station.

The FCC has been authorized by Congress to enforce U.S. Criminal Code Title 18, Section 1464, which reads, "Whoever utters any obscene, indecent, or profane language by means of radio communication shall be fined not more than $10,000 or imprisoned not more than 2 years or both." Prosecution under this section is within the jurisdiction of the Department of Justice, but the FCC is authorized to revoke a broadcast license or impose a fine for violation of Section 1464, regardless of whether there has been criminal prosecution.

The word "profane" was interpreted in Duncan vs. United States (1931) when the Circuit Court of Appeals upheld the conviction of a broadcaster who used God's name in an irreverant manner. Profane was defined as, "Irreverant toward God or holy things; speaking or spoken, acting or acted, in manifest or implied contempt of sacred things; blasphemous as profane language; profane swearing."

In the case FCC vs. Pacifica Foundation (1978), the term "indecent" was interpreted as "the concept of indecent is intimately connected with the exposure of children to language that describes, in terms patently offensive as measured by contemporary community standards for the broadcast medium, sexual or excretory activities and organs at times of the day when there is a reasonable risk that children may be in the audience."

The Supreme Court found that the First Amendment does not prohibit all governmental regulations of that which is vulgar, offensive, and shocking on the airwaves. The Congress and the Supreme Court, therefore, have authorized the FCC to enforce the laws against the pandering of the indecent, vulgar, and obscene.

We propose, therefore, the following course of action relative to the FCC. When an obscene or indecent rock 'n' roll song is heard on a local rock station, send a letter to the chairman of the FCC, Washington, DC 20554, and protest such filth on public airwaves. Give the call letters of the station along with city and state, name of the song and date and time when played. Tell the chairman that you would appreciate your letter being placed in the files of the particular radio station and that you would appreciate a letter from the FCC when the station's license is up for renewal. All drug-related songs should also be protested to the FCC. An excellent case can be made against renewal of license if the station can be convicted of pushing drugs through its music. The FCC issued a memorandum to radio stations in March and April of 1971 warning them of drug-oriented song lyrics. A carbon copy of your letter should be sent to the owner of the radio station. Most owners do not want to rock the boat with the FCC, so your letter will not go unnoticed. Ten or fifteen letters complaining about the same station will certainly gain the owner's attention. In fact, the FCC encourages listeners to write to management personnel at local stations. Says the FCC, "They are the people who are responsible for selecting the programs and announcements that are broadcast. Communications in writing to stations and networks help to keep broadcasters informed about community needs and interests as well as audience opinions on specific material."

Another approach that is sometimes effective is contacting or writing the sponsors of the station and complaining about the filth being disseminated over the airwaves and paid for by XYZ company. Most presidents of companies sponsoring ads on a radio station want to maintain proper community relationships, and your concern about drugs and X-rated materials being broadcast at their expense will at least make them sit up and take notice. If a sponsor is the local "headshop," you can forget this approach; but if respectable companies are involved, you might make an appointment with the presidents and show them the materials being broadcast. If they think the message of "Get Down Make Love" by Queen is fine, you probably don't want their products anyway. We know that Procter and Gamble agreed not to sponsor certain television programs because of an overabundance of sex and violence. Such action gives hope that sponsoring companies will listen to the public.

If local rock stations refuse to broadcast all drug and X-rated materials, there would be a shock wave felt throughout the whole industry. Unfortunately, the reverse is presently occurring. *Parents haven't been listening.* Once the station owners realize parents are listening and reporting their drug and X-rated songs to the FCC and/or sponsors, things could change in a hurry. Tell the station owners that we are acting to protect our children, since, unlike X-rated movies and books, X-rated music is available to any listener regardless of age. We are, in effect, protesting the rape of our children's minds and morals.

Write your local representative and senator and tell them you feel that the time is ripe for a full investigation into the adverse effects rock music is having on our youth, particularly in the area of drugs. Remind your elected representative that former Senator James Buckley on November 21, 1973, discussed on the Senate floor the major findings of a forty-page investigative report linking the drug epidemic to the rock industry.

The situation is twice as serious and critical today as in 1973.

If your son or daughter walked the rock music/drug highway and committed suicide, and you would be willing to so testify before a congressional hearing, an FCC hearing, or appear on such programs as the "Phil Donahue Show" to tell your story, please let me know.[12] This type of personal testimony is very effective and helps raise the level of public awareness of the issue. Unless we do, CBS Records, RCA, Warner Brothers, and the other producers of rock records will continue to pour raw sewage into our young people's minds.

Write to the following record companies reminding them of their contribution to the moral decline of our nation. Warner Brothers and CBS Records continue to produce rock's most objectionable materials. Among others, Warner's produced Frank Zappa's "The Mothers," Prince's "Dirty Mind," Exile's "I Want To Kiss You All Over," and Alice Cooper's "I Love The Dead".

CBS Records produced Tosh's "Legalize It," Pink Floyd's "The Wall," Dr. Hook's "Sloppy Seconds," Ted Nugent's "Scream Dream," and Ian Dury and the Blockheads' "Laughter". Many of the Beatles' drug songs were cut by Capitol Records.

Warner Brothers's address is 3300 Warner Boulevard, Burbank, CA 91510. CBS's address is 51 West 52nd Street, New York, NY 10019. Capitol's address is 1750 N. Fine, Hollywood, CA 90028.

Atlantic Records, producers of Alice Cooper's "Cold Ethyl" and the Rolling Stones' "Some Girls," is located at 75 Rockefeller Plaza, New York, NY 10019. Cassablanca Records, 8255 Sunset Boulevard, Los Angeles, CA 90046, produced KISS' *Plaster Caster* and Village People's *Cruising* album.

Electra/Asylum produced Queen's "Get Down Make Love" and Billy Thorpe's "In My Room." They may be reached at 962 North LaCienega, Los Angeles, CA 90069. RCA should be asked why it would produce Lou Reed's "Rock 'n' Roll Animal" record pushing heroin and marijuana. The address is 1133 Avenue of the Americas, New York, NY 10036.

While protesting the corruption and drug messages we should encourage these record companies to emphasize the "higher, purer, and warmer" themes of life. God, home, country, true love, caring, faithfulness, work ethic, study ethic, honesty are in. Perversion of all forms is out.

Don't be fooled by the record companies' claim that certain drug songs and/or albums are 1960 or 1970 vintage. These materials are still being produced and sold today! The Beatles drug albums produced by Capitol are selling more today than when they were first produced (except for *Sgt. Pepper's,* which sold over 7 million copies in 1967 and 3 million more the next year).

Also, be alert to the possibility of one "harmless" song on an album being played on the air in order to encourage your child to purchase the album only to find that the rest of the album is a moral zero.

If you live near a rock recording company, consider this suggestion from a former employee. Since drugs are so much a part of the industry, you could nearly grind the operation to a halt by having the police department turn loose their drug-sniffing dogs on the premises. Few rock bands can record without drugs. Daily raids and jail sentences for offenders would soon put a crimp in the industry.

Avoid all rock concerts, including the ones in public facilities. Cities and counties did not build those facilities for illegal drug activity. When you hear of a rock concert, encourage the police to arrest those breaking the law.

Insist that your high school and junior high school not play rock at lunch time, on buses coming to or going from the school, or at school functions. Schools with a drug problem sometimes feed the problem by keeping students high on drug music.

If your children are using allowance money to buy rock records, cut their allowance. Why should parents pay for records that tell their children to rebel against their parents?

If your children's schools are drug centers, meet with the administration, faculty, and other parents and take action. HEW's *Parents, Peers, and Pot* contains a plan of action for parents. Texan's War On Drugs, 7171 Forest Lane, Dallas, Texas 75230, has excellent materials and ideas for combating this situation. Insist that drug laws be strictly enforced and that major drug pushers receive maximum sentences.

Taiwan had a heroin problem until it began to hang heroin pushers. Dr. Hardin Jones in his book *Sensual Drugs* insists that marijuana is the most dangerous illegal drug.[13] Major marijuana pushers should expect to receive the same consideration that heroin pushers received in Taiwan.

Music is only part of the problem—albeit a major part since its influence is so powerful—we should also consider the influence of modern art, films, and literature.

Why not avoid modern art museums and displays? We certainly don't have to buy and give respectabil' to chaotic and meaningless art. Paint thrown on car or wood run over with automobiles or bikes is not art. We should display meaningful art and art of good taste. God's creation (which includes us and our works) is infinite, purposeful, harmonious, beautiful. Display beauty instead of glorifications of the ugly.

Say "no" to movies of violence, immorality, and profane language. Voice your protest when anti-Christian films are screened. Likewise, thank the owners and management for decent films like *Sound of Music.*

Teenagers did not foist this evil upon themselves. Adult men and women strapped this monkey on their backs, and it will take men and women of goodwill to unstrap it. Most teenagers have a difficult enough time working out their own identity, world view, sexuality, and lifestyle without the constant pull of the rock industry encouraging them to try sex, drugs, perversion, and anarchy.

Our Lord warns against corrupting children (Matthew 18:6), and yet rock 'n' roll by its very nature is a corruption of youth. Jeff Greenfield in his work *No Peace, No Place* said that rock music to a twelve- or thirteen-year-old is a music of unbearable sexuality. "We are the first to have our music rooted in uncoated sexuality."[14] Our children are being seduced and molested by the rock world. Galatians 5:19–21 and 2 Peter 2 identify this rock world and its nature.

One further suggestion. Because many Christian and non-Christian teens are already hooked by the rock/drugs/sex matrix they may need to enroll for an intensive two-week seminar at The Summit,[15] where these issues are faced within the context of the Christian world view. It has been our experience that most Christian young people are helped tremendously when they discover the role played by rock 'n' roll in the struggle between Christianity and an atheistic, hedonistic world view. Even non-Christians can understand the debilitating effects of the rock, drug, sex lifestyle. Sometimes it just needs to be pointed out under the right conditions. Then, too, some parents have already lost communication with their teenagers. The Summit fills this gap. Also, non-Christians can be won over to a Christian lifestyle when the Gospel of Jesus Christ is presented in contrast to the gospel of John Lennon and the whole rock 'n' roll lifestyle. The Summit offers a vivid look at the alternatives teenagers face while presenting Christ and the Christian life as the most satisfying and ultimately correct position worth living.

Carl F. H. Henry summarized the alternatives as, "The final choice for modern man is between Christianity and nihilism, between the Logos of God (Christ) and the ultimate meaninglessness of life and the world."[16]

Conclusion

Young men and women just learning to cope with their own sexuality, totally oblivious of the enormous price they are paying for their continuing love affair with rock 'n' roll, are being exploited and manipulated by clever musical pornographers.

Millions of young people are enslaved by the drug culture and by listening carefully to Pink Floyd's "The Wall" suggesting suicide, the Village People preaching homosexuality, Prince advocating incest and lewdness, Alice Cooper singing about making love to the dead, and Dr. Hook making love to boys and animals. There are no taboos, no rules, no laws. And there is no true and satisfying love. While some lyrics capitulate in concept to true love, the music expresses unspoken desires to smash true love to pieces.

Our teenagers hardly stand a chance!

Even though rock 'n' roll has been with us for more than a quarter of a century, its cultural score card rates zero. Rock is a blight on America's youth. Nearly everything rock touches or advocates is repugnant to good taste, mental and physical health, and spiritual well-being. It is the exact opposite of "the warmer, higher and purer" qualities of music spoken of by Solzhenitsyn.

Rock has turned our young women into sex machines, our young men into lust mongers.

It has degraded love, sex, and marriage and upgraded lasciviousness. It has made a mockery of morality while encouraging fornication, bisexuality, and homosexuality.

And while attacking God, Jesus Christ, the Bible, and Christianity, it has sympathized with the Devil and opened the door to the occult and paganism.

It has alienated children from parents and widened the generation gap. It has downgraded patriotism and preached violent revolution. It has tarnished our nation's culture and promoted and sustained the drug counter-culture.

The rock industry is a moral, cultural, and spiritual wasteland. It has no redeeming social value.

Verification comes from within the rock world. Lisa Robinson, long time observer and pro-rock writer said,

> There's gonorrhea, syphilis, crabs, NSU, venereal warts and herpes to consider. . . I mean, you'd be simply amazed at the number of times one has to schlepp to the VD clinic; it's almost a regular stop for some groups on the way to or from a gig [a rock concert]. . . . The intrigue, the search, the wallowing through the muck and mire of sleeze is all part of it. It's all part of the rock and roll lifestyle, isn't it?[1]

In spite of such total degradation, however, rock continues to claim young people for its one-way, downhill ride. "After three months researching rock," said a newspaper reporter,

> I'm convinced the stars have the morals of a rabbit hutch. Compared to the private lives of the Beatles and the Rolling Stones, members of the Jet Set are so many Victorian tea-party cookie pushers.[2]

CONCLUSION

Rock singer Mackenzie Phillips has the honesty to say of her own father, John Phillips, of both the original and reformed rock group, the Mamas and the Papas, "I have always felt very positive about my father even though he was a junkie and a slimy person."[3] Phillips started with marijuana and psychedelics in the 1960s, went into cocaine with the Hollywood Snort Set in early '70s, and graduated to heroin in 1976 knowing full well the drug-related deaths of Hendrix, Morrison, Joplin, and others.

Sexual promiscuity, alternative lifestyles, and drugs may seem right to many, but the bottom line continues to register another verdict. Experimenting with unrestricted hedonism has its consequences—heartache, suffering, disease, and death.

For those skeptics who scoff at such an extreme conclusion, research Altamont![4] Look at Janis Joplin, Jimi Hendrix, Keith Moon, Brian Jones, Bon Scott! Lou Reed said his fans would rather see him die than turn his back on heroin and the drug lifestyle.[5]

The Bible teaches that nations and civilizations practicing the lifestyle advocated by rock 'n' roll do not prosper or progress.[6]

"The more sexually permissive a society becomes," said Dr. J. D. Unwin, "the less creative energy it exhibits and the slower its movement toward rationality, philosophical speculation, and advanced civilization."[7] Unwin studied eighty primitive and civilized societies and discovered a *distinct correlation between increasing sexual freedom and social decline.*

Harvard sociologist Pitirim Sorokin wrote in his *The American Sexual Revolution* that "there is no example of a community which has retained its high position on the cultural scale after less rigorous sexual customs have replaced more restricting ones."[8] He also observed that immoral and antisocial behavior increases with cultural permissiveness toward the erotic sub-arts. Lennon's erotic sub-arts only verify Sorokin's contention.

Bruno Bettelheim said, "If a society does not taboo sex, children will grow up in relative sex freedom. But so far, history has shown that such a society cannot create culture or civilization; it remains primitive."[9]

Arnold Toynbee said that a culture which postpones rather than stimulates sexual experience in young adults is a culture most prone to progress.[10]

It should be obvious by now that my point of reference for John Lennon, his legacy, and rock 'n' roll in general has been the biblical standard of morality. Lennon's fans who followed him closely through the drug and sex revolution will disagree with little that has been written. But they are convinced that such a lifestyle is worth living.

It is my hope to persuade some that drugs and promiscuity are the ways of death, not life, that the biblical standard of morality is neither archaic, nor repressive, and is essential for personal growth and development.

I agree with C. S. Lewis who argued in his *Abolition of Man* that there is really only one moral order. Those living outside of it aren't creating a new moral order; rather they are simply breaking the established one.

Many years ago John Lennon's fans were screaming "We want John, not Jesus, John, not Jesus."[11] Though millions deny it, the word of John Lennon spells death, not life. The Word of Jesus Christ spells life.

The Bible says, "There is a way which seems right to a man, but its end is the way to death."[12] This verse should speak to millions, but the Bible no longer holds the influence it once did. Some say it is full of errors and contradictions. Others, if they were honest, would have to admit they never read it.

Werner Keller, a skeptic for many years, finally concluded,

> In view of the overwhelming mass of authentic and well-attested evidence now available, as I thought of the skeptical criticism which from the eighteenth century onward would fain have demolished the Bible altogether, there kept hammering in my brain this one sentence: "The Bible is right after all!"[13]

And Dr. Harold O. J. Brown came to a similiar conclusion, "It is easier to believe in the complete trustworthiness of the Bible today than at any time in the past century."[14]

W. F. Albright confirms the Bible with this statement, "Archaeology, after a long silence, has finally corroborated biblical tradition in no uncertain way."[15]

Russia's nuclear physicist B. P. Dotsenko found the gospel of our Lord Jesus Christ in a hay stack in a barn and ultimately allowed its message to win him to Christ. Said Dotsenko, "I began to realize, moreover, that the most brilliant scientists in the best equipped laboratories still are incapable of copying even the simplest living cell. I started to pray and to worship God."[16]

"A young man who wishes to remain a sound atheist," said C. S. Lewis, "cannot be too careful of his reading. There are traps everywhere—Bibles laid open . . ."[17]

Lewis said his turning point came when he read G. K. Chesterton's book *Everlasting Man,* where he saw for the first time "the whole Christian outline of history set out in a form that seemed to me to make sense,"[18] and in hearing "the hardest boiled of all the atheists" admit that the evidence for the historicity of the Gospels was really surprisingly good and that the resurrection of Christ "almost looks as if it had really happened once."[19] It was shortly after that C. S. Lewis' atheism melted and he admitted "that God was God, and knelt and prayed."[20] Said Lewis, he was probably "the most dejected and reluctant convert in all England. But who can duly adore that Love which will open the high gates to a prodigal who is brought in kicking, struggling, resentful, and darting his eyes in every direction for a chance of escape?"[21]

Another longtime atheist and friend of Bertrand Russell, C. E. M. Joad, came to Christ when he realized what the Bible had to say about sin was correct. Joad finally realized that blaming society for evil wasn't the answer. Rather the human heart was the problem, and Christ is the solution. "I now believe," said Joad, "that the balance of reasoned considerations tells heavily in favour of the religious, even of the Christian view of the world."[22]

Katherine Tait, housewife, also "found it easier to believe in a universe created by an eternal God than in one that had 'just happened.'"[23] But Tait is no ordinary housewife. She is the daughter of one of this century's most famous unbelievers, Bertrand Russell.

It is no accident that we conclude with her example since Bertrand Russell was one of John Lennon's favorite writers.[24] Instead of reading the father's *Why I Am Not a Christian,* Lennon should have tried the daughter's version of *Why I Am!* She tells of her spiritual rebirth in her book *My Father Bertrand Russell.*

CONCLUSION

Original sin, forgiveness and grace were like "sun-shine after long days of rain," she said.

> As I went deeper and deeper into religion, however, I found it ever more satisfying. I wished I could convince my father that it added to all I had learned from him and took very little away. I did not find it a denial of life, a brier patch of restrictions, but a joyful affirmation. 'I am come that they might have life and have it more abundantly,' said Jesus . . . I was already bound by the exacting moral code my father had taught me that I saw no new restrictions in Christianity, merely the possibility of living with those I already had.[25]

Had John Lennon lived, he too might have been led to see that Jesus Christ alone gives meaning to life. Bob Dylan came to this conclusion, and he now sings, "There's only one road, and it leads to Calvary," and even Woody Guthrie's son, Arlo, now says he is "pursuing God at a deadly pace." Lennon already was willing to admit error in his earlier radicalism. He already was beginning to see the dead end of promiscuity. He eventually might have publicly confessed that his way was the way of Altamont, Gadara, Gulag, and Gehenna!

He may have ultimately agreed with Renan who said, "Among the sons of men there has not appeared a greater than the son of Mary."[26] Or with H. G. Wells who once said, "Is it any wonder that to this day this Galilean is too much for our small hearts."[27]

Lennon should have seriously considered the words of a fellow Britisher, who, though an atheist, announced,

> It was reserved for Christianity to present to the world an ideal character, which through all the changes of eighteen centuries, has filled the hearts of men with an impassioned love; and has shown itself capable of acting

on all ages, nations, temperaments, and conditions: and has not only been the highest pattern of virtue, but the highest incentive to its practice; and has exerted so deep an influence that it may be truly said that the simple record of three short years of active life has done more to regenerate and soften mankind than all the disquisitions of philosophers, and than all the exhortations of moralists. This has been the well-spring of whatever is best and purest in the Christian life.[28]

We must all believe in someone and something. We all stake our lives on what we believe. The Bible says, "Believe on the Lord Jesus Christ."

When the Bible says believe on the Lord Jesus Christ and thou shalt be saved, it means saved from sin and hell; it means a life of purpose; it means heaven.

The Bible says, "Taste and see that the Lord is good." To slightly revise a song—"Give Jesus Christ a Chance."

Once to every man and nation
Comes the moment to decide
In the strife of Truth with Falsehood,
For the good or evil side.
Then it is the brave man chooses,
While the coward stands aside.

James Russell Lowell

NOTES

Introduction
 1. *Playboy,* January 1981, p. 89.
 2. *Penthouse,* October 1969, p. 34.
 3. Colorado Springs (Colorado) *Sun,* March 15, 1981, p. 4A.
 4. *Playboy,* January 1981, p. 89.
 5. *Tulsa World,* December 12, 1980, p. 1C.
 6. *Human Events,* March 14, 1981, p. 12.
 7. David A. Noebel, *Rock 'n' Roll: A Prerevolutionary Form of Cultural Subversion* (Manitou Springs, Colo.: Summit Press, 1980), p. 6.
 8. *The New York Times,* December 14, 1980, p. 42.
 9. *Chicago Tribune,* September 3, 1966, p. 3.
 10. Jann Wenner, *Lennon Remembers* (New York: Fawcett Popular Library, 1971), p. 87.
 11. Ibid.
 12. *A Tribute To John Lennon* was published by *US* magazine, 215 Lexington Ave., New York, NY 10016. The quote is on p. 35.
 13. Cynthia Lennon, *A Twist Of Lennon* (New York: Avon Books, 1980), p. 141.

Chapter One
 1. *Newsweek,* September 1, 1980, p. 48. These figures, according to *Newsweek,* are based on a recent new study by Johns Hopkins University professors Melvin Zelnik and John F. Kantner.
 2. *Time,* April 6, 1981, p. 21.
 3. *Newsweek,* September 1, 1980, p. 48. See also *Time,* August 2, 1982. This issue contains a five-page report on herpes referring to it as the scourge, the Scarlet Letter, the VD of the Ivy League and Jerry Falwell's revenge. According to *Time* the herpes epi-

demic is the result of two decades of "sexual permissiveness." Rock 'n' roll has preached sexual permissiveness for two decades.

4. A 1975 Massachusetts study found that one out of every six drivers responsible for a fatal accident was high on marijuana when the accident occurred. A 1975 California study found that one in seven traffic deaths was the result of a stoned driver. And marijuana potency has *increased* since 1975. Dashboard pipes, sold at drug paraphernalia stores, enable the marijuana smoker to smoke and drive at the same time. For further information on drug related deaths, write Texans' War on Drugs Committee, 7171 Forest Lane, Dallas, TX 75230 or call (214) 661-6180.

5. Peggy Mann, "Frightening Facts about Children and Drugs," *Family Weekly,* November 25, 1979, p. 6. Reprint by permission of FAMILY WEEKLY, copyright 1979, 641 Lexington Avenue, New York, New York 10022.

6. Ibid.

7. *Newsweek,* November 12, 1979, p. 107.

8. *Dallas Morning News,* October 29, 1978, p. 14A.

9. Jonathan Eisen, ed., *The Age of Rock: Sounds of the American Cultural Revolution* (New York: Random House, 1969), p. 61.

10. *Seattle Post-Intelligencer,* April 12, 1980, p. 8B.

11. McCandlish Phillips, *The Bible, the Supernatural, and the Jews* (Minneapolis: Bethany Fellowship, Inc., 1970), p. 272.

12. Ibid.

13. *Tampa Tribune,* August 21, 1981, p. 8D.

14. Ibid.

15. *Washington Post,* February 6, 1980, p. 10.

16. *Tulsa Tribune,* November 17, 1978, p. 7A.

17. *Republic,* bk. III, p. 401.

18. Jacques Barzun, *Darwin, Marx, Wagner* (New York: Doubleday and Co., 1958), p. 231.

19. *The Cleveland Press,* July 25, 1969, p. 1N.

20. *Newsweek,* April 2, 1979, p. 58.

21. Eisen, ed. *The Age of Rock,* p. 190.

22. C.S. Lewis, *God in the Dock* (Grand Rapids: Wm. B. Eerdmans Publishing Co., 1971), p. 262.

Chapter Two

1. *Dallas Times Herald,* October 29, 1978. He also said in this interview with Jere Longman that rock is not from God. The lyrics don't talk about Jesus and the beat hypnotizes. Little Richard (Richard Penniman) now says his rock 'n' roll days of

NOTES

"Tutti Frutti," "Long Tall Sally," "Rip It Up," and "Good Golly Miss Molly" were days of insanity.

2. *The Dallas Morning News,* October 29, 1978, p. 14A.
3. Brian Epstein, the Beatles manager, was a homosexual who died of an overdose of drugs (carbrital) on August 27, 1967, at the age of thirty-two. Worth $14 million, he became a victim of his own sub-culture. Said Lennon, "Brian was very hard to live with, he had a lot of tantrums and things like that, like most fags do, you know, they are very insecure." Jann Wenner, *Lennon Remembers* (New York: Fawcett Popular Library, 1971), p. 83. In *Playboy,* January, 1981, p. 107, Lennon described Brian Epstein's sex life as a nice "Hollywood Babylon." He also said it was his first experience with someone he knew to be a homosexual. *New York Times* writer McCandlish Phillips observed, "Brian Epstein became, in a sense, the father of a generation. Today there are scores of groups of similar or imitative mode, many plugging Satan's message, and some are of appalling depravity. With it Brian Epstein got the kind of packages the devil loves to give: fast, short-term thrills and rewards, with enough poison thrown in to send him into the grave at thirty-two." McCandlish Phillips, *The Bible, the Supernatural, and the Jews* (Minneapolis: Bethany Fellowship, Inc., 1970), p. 297.
4. *Dallas Times Herald,* October 29, 1978.
5. From Lennon's "I Am The Walrus."
6. Tony Sanchez, *Up and Down with the Rolling Stones* (New York: Wm. Morrow and Co., 1979), p. 212.
7. Bob Larson, *Rock* (Wheaton, Ill.: Tyndale House Publishers, Inc., 1980), p. 122.
8. *Kansas City Times,* August 24, 1979, p. 6C.
9. McCandlish Phillips, *The Bible, the Supernatural, and the Jews* (Minneapolis: Bethany Fellowship, Inc., 1970), p. 294.
10. Ibid.
11. *Rolling Stone,* February 12, 1976, p. 83.
12. Ibid., p. 87.
13. Ibid.
14. Ibid., p. 92.
15. Ibid.
16. Ibid., p. 100.
17. Ibid., pp. 92, 94.
18. Steve Stone, *John Lennon: All You Need Is Love,* MarJam, Box 3166, NY 10163, p. 86.
19. *The American Journal of Psychiatry,* vol. 99, p. 317.
20. *Seattle Daily Times,* August 22, 1964, p. 1.

21. *Los Angeles Herald-Examiner,* August 8, 1965, p. 9J. Reprinted with permission of the Editor of the Los Angeles Herald-Examiner.
22. *The American Journal of Psychiatry,* vol. 101, p. 364.
23. *Wichita Beacon,* February 17, 1965, p. 11A. Dr. William Sargant's book *Battle for the Mind* was published by Doubleday and Co., 1957.
24. *Time,* September 22, 1967, p. 60.
25. Ibid.
26. *Tulsa World,* December 12, 1980, p. 20.

Chapter Three
1. Jann Wenner, *Lennon Remembers* (New York: Fawcett Popular Library, 1971), p. 168. Herbert Read said of Duchamp, "Duchamp's original purpose was not to deceive the spectator: he is an iconoclast and his purpose is to destroy the whole academic concept of a 'work' of art . . . A urinal, from this point of view, is just as valid as the Venus de Milo." Herbert Read, *A Concise History of Modern Painting* (New York: Frederick A. Praeger, 1968), p. 268.
2. H.R. Rookmaaker, *Modern Art and the Death of a Culture* (Downers Grove, Ill.: InterVarsity Press, 1971), p. 126.
3. Ibid.
4. Ibid., p. 220.
5. *The Pensacola News-Journal,* April 1, 1979, p. 21A.
6. *Tulsa World,* February 10, 1979, p. 6A.
7. Ibid.
8. Duncan Williams, *Trousered Apes* (New Rochelle, N.Y.: Arlington House, 1972), p. 40.
9. Ibid., p. 60.
10. Ibid., pp. 61, 62.
11. Ibid., Foreword to the American edition.
12. James C. Hefley, *Textbooks on Trial* (Wheaton, Ill.: Scripture Press Publications, 1976), p. 175. The book is now available from The Mel Gablers, P.O. Box 7518, Longview, TX 75607.
13. Ibid., p. 160.
14. Rookmaaker, *Modern Art,* p. 205.
15. Ibid., p. 222.
16. Steve Stone, *John Lennon: All You Need Is Love,* MarJam, Box 3166, NY 10163, p. 27.
17. *Art In America,* May-June 1978, p. 103.
18. Rookmaaker, *Modern Art,* p. 130.
19. *Playboy,* January 1981, p. 110.
20. Margaret E. Stucki, *The Revolutionary Mission of Modern Art*

(Cape Canaveral, Fla.: Birds' Meadow Publishing Co., 1973), p. 30. This excellent volume is available from Summit Press, Box 207, Manitou Springs, CO 80829. Stucki traces the atheistic influence on modern art much like we are seeking to do with modern music. The parallels are not only striking, but identical. For Picasso's quote and pro-Marxist stance see also Herbert Read, *A Concise History of Modern Painting,* p. 160.

21. Ibid., p. 16. Read also explained the basis of the future civilization in these words, "To present a clear and distinct visual image of sensuous experience—that has always been the undeviating aim of these artists [Picasso, Kandinsky, Klee, Mondrian, Pollock], and the rich treasury of icons they have created is the basis upon which any possible civilization of the future will be built." Read, *Concise History,* p. 290.
22. Ibid., p. 15.
23. Ibid., p. 21.
24. Ibid., pp. 19, 20.
25. Rookmaaker, *Modern Art,* pp. 188, 189.
26. Francis A. Schaeffer, *How Should We Then Live?* (Old Tappan, N.J.: Fleming H. Revell Company, 1976), p. 184.
27. Ibid., p. 194.
28. Ibid.
29. Ibid., p. 193.
30. Ibid., p. 197.
31. Malcolm Muggeridge, *The End of Christendom* (Grand Rapids: Wm. B. Eerdmans Publishing Co., 1980), p. 18.
32. Ibid., p. 17.

Chapter Four
1. Alfred J. Aronowitz, "The Return of the Beatles," *The Saturday Evening Post,* August 8, 1964, p. 25. Reprinted from *The Saturday Evening Post,* © 1964 The Curtis Publishing Company.
2. Ibid., p. 28.
3. Jann Wenner, *Lennon Remembers* (New York: Fawcett Popular Library, 1971), p. 130.
4. *People,* February 23, 1981, p. 40.
5. *Newsweek,* September 3, 1979, p. 65.
6. *Time,* September 17, 1979, p. 101.
7. *Rolling Stone,* April 30, 1981, p. 31.
8. *Time,* October 20, 1975, p. 62. Said *Time,* " 'Lisztomania' begins with Roger Daltrey of The Who frenetically kissing the [expletive deleted] of the Countess Marie in time to an amok metronome." *Time* also reported that Russell said, "Ok Roger, take off your clothes, get in bed and have an [expletive deleted]."

9. Anthony Hilder's review is in the author's possession.

10. *Christianity Today,* April 10, 1981, p. 85. Russell not only portrays Christianity as a myth, but final truth as a myth—"The final truth is that there is no final truth."

11. *Playboy,* February, 1965, p. 58.

12. *Washington Post,* August 15, 1966. See also *Christianity Today,* September 2, 1966, p. 54.

13. John Lennon, *A Spaniard in the Works* (New York: Simon and Schuster, 1965), p. 14.

14. Ibid.

15. Ibid., p. 90.

16. *Parade,* Sunday Supplement, June 27, 1965.

17. *San Francisco Chronicle,* April 13, 1966, p. 26.

18. Hunter Davies, *The Beatles* (New York: McGraw Hill Co., 1968), p. 210.

19. *Time,* September 5, 1968, p. 60.

20. *Playboy,* January, 1981, p. 112.

21. Ron Smith, *John Lennon: A Tribute* (New York: David Zentner Publication, 1980), p. 34.

22. John Lennon, "God," from the album *Plastic Ono Band,* 1970. First assignee of copyright, Maclen (music) Ltd. (U.K.)—B.M.I.

23. *Rolling Stone,* January 22, 1981, p. 66.

24. *Rolling Stone,* February 5, 1981, p. 14.

25. Tony Sanchez, *Up And Down With The Rolling Stones* (New York: Wm. Morrow and Co., 1979), p. 179.

26. Ibid., p. 180.

27. Ibid., p. 181.

28. Ibid.

29. Ibid., p. 185.

30. Ibid., p. 182.

31. Davies, *The Beatles,* p. 77.

32. *Parade,* October 4, 1964, p. 12.

33. Jann Wenner, *Lennon Remembers,* pp. 84, 86.

34. *Penthouse,* October, 1969, p. 32.

35. *Parade,* February 1, 1981.

36. *Tulsa Tribune,* April 12, 1969, p. 14B.

37. Reo M. Christenson, "Censorship of Pornography? Yes," *The Progressive,* September 1970, quotes J.D. Unwin and his book *Sex and Culture.*

Chapter Five

1. Steve Stone, *John Lennon: All You Need Is Love,* MarJam, Box 3166, NY 10163, p. 63f.

NOTES

2. Marsha Manatt, *Parents, Peers and Pot* (Washington, D.C.: U.S. Department of Health, Education and Welfare, 1979), p. 24.
3. Ibid.
4. David A. Noebel's *The Marxist Minstrels* is available from Summit Press, Box 207, Manitou Springs, CO 80829.
5. S. Taqi, "Approbation of Drug Usage in Rock and Roll Music," *U.N. Bulletin on Narcotics*, vol. XXI, no. 4, October–December, 1969, p. 35.
6. Steve Stone, *John Lennon: All You Need Is Love*, p. 63.
7. Gene Lees, "Rock, Violence, and Spiro T. Agnew," *High Fidelity*, February, 1970, pp. 108, 110.
8. *Rolling Stone*, January 7, 1971, p. 39. See Jann Wenner, *Lennon Remembers* (New York: Fawcett Popular Library, 1971), p. 76.
9. Ibid.
10. *Playboy*, January 1981, p. 112.
11. Wenner, *Lennon Remembers*, p. 82.
12. Ibid.
13. *Chicago Tribune*, April 27, 1980.
14. *Family Week*, November 25, 1979, p. 5.
15. *Stevenson's Book of Quotations* (New York: Dodd-Mead, 1958), p. 123.
16. *Time*, September 22, 1967, p. 62.
17. Hunter Davies, *The Beatles* (New York: McGraw Hill Co., 1968), p. 228.
18. Ibid., p. 225.
19. *Time*, September 22, 1967, p. 62.
20. *Newsweek*, July 31, 1978, p. 40.
21. *Circus*, August 3, 1973, p. 38.
22. *Central California Register*, July 6, 1967, p. 7.
23. *American Opinion*, May 1969, p. 59.
24. *Time*, September 26, 1969, p. 69.
25. *Cavalier*, February, 1969, p. 37.
26. *Cavalier*, June 1968.
27. *Life*, June 28, 1968.
28. "Sloppy Seconds," produced by Columbia Records, glamorizes cocaine, marijuana, fornication, homosexuality, bestiality and making love to the dead—a deadly potion.
29. *High Times*, October, 1977, p. 46. Used by permission.
30. *People*, August 28, 1978, p. 72.
31. *TV Guide*, July 29, 1978, p. 21.
32. *Parade*, March 2, 1980, p. 16.
33. *Daily Cardinal*, December 3, 1968, p. 5.
34. Davies, *The Beatles*, p. 281.

35. *Life,* June 16, 1967, p. 105.
36. Davies, *The Beatles,* p. 310.
37. Ibid., p. 78.
38. Ibid.
39. *Tulsa World,* July 25, 1967, p. 13.
40. Davies, *The Beatles,* p. 272.
41. Ibid., p. 289.
42. Ibid., p. 228.
43. Ibid., p. 235.
44. *Tulsa World,* April 1, 1969, p. 3.
45. *Penthouse,* October, 1969, p. 29.
46. *Commonweal,* May 12, 1967, p. 235.
47. *Time,* September 26, 1969, p. 69.
48. *Cavalier,* February, 1969, p. 37.
49. House Select Committee on Crime, *Crime in America—Illicit and Dangerous Drugs,* October 23–25, 27, 1969, p. 152.
50. Ibid., p. 148. When Linkletter testified in 1969, most rock 'n' roll record shops were not selling drug paraphernalia. Today they are! The head shops have moved into the record shops. Rock music and drugs have always gone together. From Presley, Little Richard, and the Beatles to the present, the situation continues to deteriorate.

Chapter Six
1. Jann Wenner, *Lennon Remembers* (New York: Fawcett Popular Library, 1971), p. 91.
2. Tony Sanchez, *Up and Down With the Rolling Stones* (New York: Wm. Morrow and Co., 1979), p. 19.
3. Ibid., p. 121.
4. Senate Internal Security Subcommittee, *Institute of Pacific Relations,* Part 13, April 1, 1952, p. 4509.
5. Sanchez, *Up and Down,* p. 121.
6. Ibid., p. 122.
7. Ibid., p. 62.
8. Ibid., p. 122.
9. Ibid.
10. McCandlish Phillips, *The Bible, the Supernatural, and the Jews* (Minneapolis: Bethany Fellowship, Inc., 1970), p. 271.
11. Sanchez, *Up and Down,* pp. 184, 185.
12. *Communist Daily World,* February 22, 1969, p. 7M.
13. Jonathan Eisen, ed., *The Age of Rock* (New York: Random House, 1969), pp. 72, 73.
14. *Insurgent,* vol. I, no. 1, March-April 1965, p. 12.
15. *Washington Star,* March 11, 1967.

NOTES

16. Wenner, *Lennon Remembers,* p. 110.
17. Ibid.
18. *Rolling Stone,* February 5, 1981, p. 14.
19. *New York Times,* December 14, 1980, p. 42.
20. *Newsweek,* September 29, 1980. p. 77.
21. Wenner, *Lennon Remembers,* p. 86.
22. *Tulsa World,* December 12, 1980, p. 2C.
23. Wenner, *Lennon Remembers,* p. 131.
24. Ibid., p. 134.
25. Ibid., p. 132.
26. *Tulsa World,* December 12, 1980, p. 1C.
27. Ron Smith, *John Lennon: A Tribute* (New York: David Zentner Publication, 1980), p. 30.
28. Ibid.
29. *Newsweek,* April 2, 1979, p. 58.
30. Wenner, *Lennon Remembers,* p. 132.
31. *Rolling Stone,* January 22, 1981, p. 70.
32. *Arkansas Democrat,* December 18, 1980.
33. *Christian Century,* January 15, 1969, p. 92.
34. *Playboy,* January, 1981, p. 89.
35. *Newsweek,* September 29, 1980, p. 77.
36. *St. Louis Globe Democrat,* September 30, 1971, p. 1B.
37. *Playboy,* January, 1981, p. 114.
38. *Penthouse,* October, 1969, p. 32.
39. Sanchez, *Up and Down,* p. 206.
40. Ibid.
41. *Manchester Union Leader,* November 14, 1966, p. 22.
42. *Congressional Record,* March 11, 1969, p. E 1898. Since this quote has been disputed, see also H. Kent Geiger's *The Family in Soviet Russia* for further information regarding the Communist use of sex for revolutionary purposes.
43. *Tulsa Tribune,* April 23, 1969, p. 18E.
44. *Riverside* (CA) *Daily Enterprise and Press,* February 11, 1969.
45. *Newsweek,* April 20, 1981, p. 106.
46. *National Review,* March 6, 1981, p. 225.
47. David A. Noebel, *Rock 'n' Roll: A Prerevolutionary Form of Cultural Subversion* (Manitou Springs, Colo.: Summit Press, 1980), p. 4.
48. *Ft. Lauderdale News,* March 6, 1969, p. 10C. The statement was made by Jim Morrison, then of The Doors. Anyone interested in further information on Morrison and The Doors may also want to read Warner Books' 1980 edition of Jerry Hopkins/Daniel Sugarman's *No One Here Gets Out Alive.*
49. *National Review,* March 6, 1981, p. 225.

50. Ibid.
51. H. Kent Geiger, *The Family in Soviet Russia* (Cambridge, Mass.: Harvard University Press, 1970), p. 36.
52. Ibid., p. 66.
53. Charles Hartshorne, *Beyond Humanism* (Gloucester, Mass.: Peter Smith, 1975), p. 63.
54. H. Kent Geiger, *The Family,* p. 68.
55. Ibid.
56. Ibid., p. 71.
57. Ibid., p. 68.
58. Ibid., p. 104.
59. Mme. Suzanne Labin, *The Hashish Trail,* U.S. Senate Committee on the Judiciary, September 12, 1972.
60. *The Worker,* March 9, 1965, p. 7. The article entitled, "Don't Throw Rocks at Rock 'n' Roll," stated, "It's time that we set out to develop a more positive evaluation of the styles, roots and future of Rock 'n' Roll . . . beneath all the juke-box jive there exists an idiom capable of narrating the millions of young lives confined to the ghettos of our city. No one should disparage the importance of Rock 'n' Roll to today's young people."
61. *Ramparts,* April 1969.
62. Jerry Rubin, *Do It!* (New York: Simon and Schuster, 1970), p. 19.
63. Ibid., p. 249.
64. *National Observer,* January 15, 1968. p. 22.
65. Ben Fong-Torres, "Grace Slick with Paul Kantner" in *The Rolling Stone Interviews* (New York: Coronet Communication, Inc., 1971), p. 447.
66. Ben Fong-Torres, "David Crosby," *Rolling Stone Interviews,* p. 410.
67. *Sing Out!,* May 1965, p. 63.
68. *The Cleveland Press,* July 25, 1969, p. 1N.

Chapter Seven
1. *Newsweek,* April 2, 1979, p. 64.
2. *Rolling Stone,* April 19, 1979, p. 13.
3. *Newsweek,* April 2, 1979, p. 63.
4. Ibid.
5. Frank M. duMas, *Gay Is Not Good* (Nashville: Thomas Nelson Publishers, 1979), p. 111.
6. *Newsweek,* April 2, 1979, p. 58.
7. Ibid., pp. 58, 59.
8. *Parade,* May 6, 1979, p. 18.
9. *Newsweek,* April 2, 1979, p. 58.

NOTES

10. Ibid., p. 57.
11. Ibid., p. 63.
12. *Playboy,* January, 1981, p. 144.
13. *San Francisco Chronicle,* October 22, 1979, p. 6.
14. *Los Angeles Times,* August 30, 1981 (part VII), p. 14.
15. *Time,* December 17, 1979, p. 89.
16. Ibid., p. 86.
17. Ibid.
18. Ibid., p. 94.
19. *Norwalk Reflector,* February 11, 1980, p. 10.
20. *Kansas City Times,* August 24, 1979, p. 6C.
21. *People,* March 30, 1981, p. 64.
22. *Wall Street Journal,* April 1, 1981, p. 14.
23. *Slash* magazine, vol. 3, no. 5, p. 85.
24. Ibid., p. 52.
25. *Los Angeles Times,* March 15, 1981, p. 78 (Calendar Section).
26. Ibid.
27. Ibid.
28. Carl F.H. Henry, *God, Revelation and Authority* (Waco, Tex.: Word Books, 1979), vol. IV., p. 23.
29. Ibid., vol. I, p. 19.
30. Leopold Tyrmand, "Toying With The Cultural Messages," *National Review,* September 5, 1980, p. 1083.
31. In *Colorado Springs Gazette Telegraph,* December 16, 1981, p. 9C.
32. *People,* February 9, 1981, p. 86. According to the *Dallas Times Herald,* April 10, 1981, p. 8A, she said, following her acquittal in the Cleveland obscenity case, "The prosecutors are the guys doing this for money. These guys are the real [deleted]."
33. Steven Stone, *John Lennon: All You Need Is Love,* p. 76.
34. *Colorado Springs Gazette Telegraph,* July 11, 1980, p. 7F.
35. Glen O'Brien, "Notes On the Neon Nihilists," *High Times,* November, 1980, p. 56.
36. "Cold Ethyl" is from Alice Cooper's album *Welcome To My Nightmare,* produced by Atlantic Recording Corp., a Warner Communications Company, 1975.
37. "I Love The Dead" is from Alice Cooper's album *The Alice Cooper Show,* produced by Warner Bros. Records, 1977.
38. Dave Marsh and Kevin Stein, *The Book of Rock Lists* (New York: Dell/Rolling Stone Press, 1981), p. 189.
39. *Through to Victory,* February, 1973, p. 12.
40. *Newsweek,* February 26, 1973, p. 9.
41. Ibid.
42. *The Dallas Morning News,* Nov. 1, 1981, p. 8F.

43. Ibid.
44. *Hit Parader,* July, 1975, p. 64.
45. Tony Sanchez, *Up And Down Down With The Rolling Stones* (New York: Wm. Morrow and Co. 1979), p. 150
46. *Colorado Springs Gazette Telegraph,* July 20, 1981, p. 7B.
47. McCandlish Phillips, *The Bible, The Supernatural, and the Jews* (Minneapolis: Bethany Fellowship, Inc., 1970), p. 208.
48. Leviticus 19:26-31, RSV.
49. Deuteronomy 18:10-14, RSV.
50. *Tulsa World,* September 19, 1978.
51. *Hit Parader,* February, 1978, p. 24.
52. Bob Larson, *Rock* (Wheaton, Ill.: Tyndale House, 1980), p. 40. David Kotzebue in his pamphlet "The Rock That Doesn't Roll: An Expose of Hidden and Overt Occultism in Much of Today's Rock Music" lists the following rock groups and rock stars with occult implications: The Beatles, The Rolling Stones, Styx, Led Zeppelin, The Police, The Doors, Pink Floyd, Linda Ronstadt, Bee Gees, John Denver, The Eagles, Electric Light Orchestra, Earth, Wind, and Fire, Fleetwood Mac, Rush, Judas Priest, Savoy Brown, AC/DC, Grateful Dead, Black Sabbath, Ozzy Osbourne, Blue Oyster Cult, Grace Slick and the Jefferson Starship, Santana, Meatloaf, Molly Hatchet, Nazareth, Iron Maiden, Kiss, Aerosmith, Black Oak Arkansas, Heart, Uriah Heep, Van Morrison, Daryl Hall, T. Rex and Todd Rundgren. Kotzebue's pamphlet is printed by Shatter the Darkness Outreach Ministers, 71 East Yale Avenue, Denver, CO 80210.
53. *Republic,* bk. IV. p. 424.
54. *Politics,* 1339a; 1340a, b.
55. *Rolling Stone,* October 7, 1976, p. 17.
56. Ibid., February 12, 1976, p. 80.
57. Ibid., February 19, 1981, p. 54.
58. *Newsweek,* December 21, 1981, p. 75.
59. *Billboard,* December 11, 1976, p. 39. Notes 59 through 63 are mentioned by Bob Larson in *Rock,* pp. 16-18.
60. *Circus,* January 31, 1976, p. 39.
61. Ibid., October 17, 1978, p. 34.
62. *People,* May 21, 1979, p. 53.
63. *Hit Parader,* September 1979, p. 31.
64. *Time,* April 28, 1967, p. 54.
65. Sara Davidson, "Rock Style: Defying The American Dream," *Harpers,* July 1969, p. 60.
66. *Time,* June 23, 1967, p. 53.
67. *Ft. Lauderdale News,* March 6, 1969, p. 10C.

68. *Newsweek,* November 6, 1967, p. 101.
69. *Rolling Stone,* November 16, 1978, p. 3.
70. David A. Noebel, *Rock 'n' Roll: A Prerevolutionary Form of Cultural Subversion* (Manitou Springs, Colo.: Summit Press, 1980), p. 5.
71. Sara Davidson, *Rock Style* p. 57.
72. *Oshkosh Daily Northwestern,* October 1, 1979, p. 5C., Ann Landers column. In her December 5, 1979, column, *(Chicago Sun Times,* p. 80) Alice Cooper defended "Cold Ethyl" by calling it a harmless number about necrophilia. Ann Landers replied, "you can call it funny if you want to Alice. I call it sick." The theme of necrophilia continues to surface as though it and incest are the last two taboos to be destroyed. In *Mother, Jugs, and Speed* (a film starring Bill Cosby and Raquel Welch) "an attendant climbs into the back of an ambulance and has sexual intercourse with the body of a woman who has just died," *Denver Post,* April 5, 1981, p. 1.
73. *TV Guide,* July 29, 1978, p. 18.
74. *U.S. News and World Report,* October 31. 1977, p. 47.
75. Ibid.
76. *The Wichita Eagle,* November 2, 1978, p. 7B.
77. Ibid.
78. Ibid.
79. *TV Guide,* July 29, 1978, p. 21.
80. *Tulsa World,* February 19, 1979, p. 8B.
81. Sanchez, *Up and Down,* p. 257.
82. *Rolling Stone,* March 27, 1975, p. 24. Quoted by Bob Larson in *Rock,* p. 28.
83. *Rolling Stone,* February 19, 1981, p. 52.
84. *Tulsa World,* February 2, 1979, p. 1B.
85. Ibid., September 19, 1978.
86. *Newsweek,* April 2, 1979, p. 63.
87. *People,* June 30, 1975, p. 60.
88. *Colorado Springs Gazette Telegraph,* February 26, 1981, p. 6A.
89. *Circus,* August 3, 1973, p. 38. Notes 89 through 91 are mentioned by Bob Larson in *Rock,* pp. 27, 28.
90. *Rolling Stone,* January 4, 1973, p. 16.
91. *Circus,* April 17, 1979, p. 16.
92. Sanchez, *Up and Down,* p. 12.
93. Peggy Mann, "Frightening Facts about Children and Drugs," *Family Weekly,* November 25, 1979, p. 6. Reprint by permission of FAMILY WEEKLY, copyright 1979, 641 Lexington Avenue, New York, New York 10022.
94. *Penthouse,* October, 1969, p. 29.

THE LEGACY OF JOHN LENNON

Chapter Eight
1. Malcolm Muggeridge's book *The End of Christendom* is published by Eerdman's Publishing Company, Grand Rapids, Mich., 1980.
2. *Newsweek,* December 21, 1981, p. 75.
3. Tony Sanchez, *Up And Down With The Rolling Stones* (New York: Wm. Morrow and Co., 1979), p. 182.
4. *Time,* April 13, 1982, p. 51, "By a curiosity of evolution, every human skull harbors a prehistoric vestige: a reptilian brain." The biblical concept of sin is replaced with an evolutionary explanation.
5. *The Tampa Tribune,* Sept. 4, 1981, p. 2D.
6. David A. Noebel's *Christian Rock: A Strategem of Mephistopheles* published by Summit Press is available from Summit Ministries, Box 207, Manitou Springs, CO 80829. The booklet contains thirty reasons why Christians should seriously question Christian rock.
7. Bob Larson, *Rock* (Wheaton, Ill.: Tyndale House, 1980).
8. John Diamond, *Your Body Doesn't Lie* (New York: Warner Books, 1979), p. 164.
9. *Denver Post,* June 21, 1970, p. 11 in magazine section. Retallack's experiments were reported on CBS Evening News October 16, 1970.
10. Ibid.
11. Ibid.
12. Please type out your son's or daughter's experience and send me a copy with as much detail as possible including dates and places. Send to Dr. David A. Noebel, Box 207, Manitou Springs, CO 80829. Recently someone sent me a song sung in an eighth grade class, Fall 1980, entitled, "Suicide is Painless." Is it any wonder that 20,000 teens commit suicide every year? (see *Los Angeles Times,* April 2, 1981, p. 8.)
13. Hardin Jones, *Sensual Drugs* (New York: Cambridge University Press, 1977), p. 250, "I believe we should look upon marijuana as the most potentially dangerous of the sensual drugs." "Sensual drugs," said Jones, "are those that the body has no need for, but that give the user a strong sense of pleasure," p. 2.
14. Jeff Greenfield, *No Peace, No Place* (Garden City, N. Y.: Doubleday, 1973), p. 29.
15. Summit Ministries brochures are available at Box 207, Manitou Springs, CO 80829. Telephone (303) 685-9103.
16. Carl F. H. Henry, *God, Revelation and Authority* (Waco, Tex.: Word Books, 1976), vol. I, p. 41.

NOTES

Conclusion

1. *Creem,* October 1975.
2. *St. Louis Globe Democrat,* September 28, 1971, p. 1B.
3. *People,* March 2, 1981, p. 25.
4. Tony Sanchez, *Up And Down With The Rolling Stones* (New York: Wm. Morrow and Co., 1979), pp. 179–89.
5. *People,* March 30, 1981, p. 65. The complete statement reads, "Reed realizes that his new, mellower lifestyle may not please old fans. He understands those who say 'I wish Lou Reed would write some more drug songs,' but giving in is no longer an option. 'The fans would be far happier if I died,' he observes wryly. 'That would have completed the Lou Reed myth perfectly. But I'm not about to kill him off just yet.'"
6. Leviticus 18, for example, is a judgment on Egypt and Canaan for practicing incest, adultery, child sacrifice, homosexuality, and bestiality.
7. Reo M. Christenson, "Censorship of Pornography? Yes," *The Progressive,* September 1970. Christenson quotes from Unwin's *Sex and Culture.* Christenson's article is reprinted as Exhibit A in a report of Charles H. Keating, Jr., Commission on Obscenity and Pornography, September 30, 1970. Keating's address is 18th floor, Provident Tower, Cincinnati, OH 45202.
8. Ibid., quoted from Pitirim Sorokin, *The American Sexual Revolution* (Boston: Porter Sargent, 1956).
9. Ibid.
10. Ibid., *New York Times,* May 10, 1964.
11. *Denver Post,* August 11, 1966, p. 65.
12. Proverbs 14:12, RSV
13. Werner Keller, *The Bible as History,* (New York: Wm. Morrow and Co., Apollo, 1964), p. xviii.
14. Harold O.J. Brown, *The Protest of a Troubled Protestant* (New Rochelle, N.Y.: Arlington House, 1969), p. 174.
15. William F. Albright, *The Archaeology of Palestine,* A Pelican Book (Baltimore: Penguin Books, Inc., 1960), p. 123–24.
16. B.P. Dotsenko, "From Communism to Christianity," *Christianity Today,* January 5, 1973, p. 5.
17. C.S. Lewis, *Surprised by Joy,* (New York: Harcourt, Brace and World, Inc., Harvest Book, 1958), p. 191.
18. Ibid., p. 223.
19. Ibid., p. 224.
20. Ibid., p. 228.
21. Ibid., p. 229.

155

22. C.E.M. Joad, *The Recovery of Belief* (London: Faber and Faber, Ltd., 1952), p. 22.
23. Katherine Tait, *My Father Bertrand Russell* (New York: Harcourt, Brace, Jovanovich, 1975), p. 186.
24. *Life,* June 16, 1967, p. 105. Lennon also enjoyed reading Allen Ginsburg and Paul Tillich.
25. Katherine Tait, *My Father Bertrand Russell,* p. 189.
26. James D. Bales, *Communism and the Reality of Moral Law* (Nutley, N.J.: Craig Press, 1969), p. 193. The quote is found in Renan's book, *Man, Real, and Ideal.*
27. H.G. Wells, *The Outline of History* (New York: Garden City Publishing Co., 1929), pp. 504–5.
28. W.E.H. Lecky, *History of European Morals from Augustus to Charlemagne,* II:8. Quoted by Bales, *Communism,* pp. 193–94.

Index

INDEX

INDEX

Townshend, Peter, 90
Toynbee, Arnold, 136
Travolta, John, 103
Two Virgins, The, 52, 74, 75, 76, 81, 89
Tyrmand, Leopold, 94

U

U.N. Bulletin on Narcotics, 56
Unwin, J.D., 53, 119, 135
U.S. Department of Health, Education and Welfare, 56, 115, 129

V

van den Haag, Dr. Ernest, 81, 82
Van Gogh, Vincent, 33
Van Halen, 20
Vicious, Sid, 96, 118
Village People, 87, 88, 108, 128, 133
Voidoids, 97, 121

W

"Wall, The," 97, 111, 127, 133

Warner Brothers, 45, 98, 108, 127
Warner Communications, 100, 121
Wagner, Richard, 23
Webb, Sidney, 70
"Well Well Well," 50
Wells, H.G., 139
White Album, 66, 72, 102
"White Rabbit," 59, 62
Who, The, 26, 44, 45, 90, 91, 118, 145
Williams, Prof. Duncan, 35, 36
Williams, Wendy O., 96
Williams, Wheeler, 39
Wolff, Lester, 18, 59
"Working Class Hero," 73, 74, 75, 76, 79
Wyman, Phil, 103, 104

Y

"Yellow Submarine," 58, 66
"YMCA," 88

Z

Zappa, Frank, 44, 62, 76, 127
Zelnik, Melvin, 141